Praise for
Godonomics

"*Godonomics* is a thoughtful critique of the theories that control the world of commerce and shape the lives of men and nations. Chad Hovind challenges us to reassess doing business as usual."

> —DR. PETER A. LILLBACK, president of Westminster
> Theological Seminary, Philadelphia

"Chad Hovind offers a creative and compelling case for the constitutional framework for government. He also provides practical financial principles that will help you make wise decisions with your money."

> —SHANE F. KRAUSER, author of *Your Nation to Save*
> and director of the American Academy for Constitutional
> Education

"A truly brilliant breakdown of what the Bible says about the economy. *Godonomics* touches on everything from profit and charity to capitalism and taxes. Everyone should get a copy."

> —GOVERNOR MIKE HUCKABEE, host of television's *Huckabee*

"*Godonomics* is an incredible comparison of biblical economics and the culture. A real eye-opener."

> —JOSH D. MCDOWELL, popular speaker and coauthor
> of *Undaunted* and *The Unshakable Truth*

"Chad Hovind brings a reasonable voice to the convinced and the unconvinced. *Godonomics* applies God's wisdom on economics both to individuals and nations. You will learn about the Bible's prescription to secure our nation's future economic health."

> —DAVID BARTON, founder and president of WallBuilders

"Simple enough to teach kids but researched enough for *The Wall Street Journal*. *Godonomics* is the truth project of economics."

—Bob McEwen, former six-term member of Congress
and popular lecturer on free-market economics

"Using God's Word regarding financial principles, you can now be bold in speaking out against false teachings. Your entire family will learn from this important book."

—Mark Whitacre, PhD, president of operations and COO
of Cypress Systems, Inc.

"*Godonomics* is thought-provoking, courageous, and relevant. Pastor Hovind, in this brilliant work, causes us to remember that 'In God We Trust.'"

—Reverend C. L. Bryant, former NAACP chapter president,
FreedomWorks fellow, and creator of the documentary film
Runaway Slave

"Chad Hovind reveals how the Bible supports free enterprise and entrepreneurship. You'll laugh and learn as he weaves together biblical history, philosophy, and a passion for business with references to Adam Smith, C. S. Lewis, Milton Friedman, and even Steve Martin."

—Glenn Beck, host of *The Glenn Beck Program* and author of
Cowards: What Politicians, Radicals, and the Media Refuse to Say

"*Godonomics* reveals an approach to money and our country that is common sense, not just another attempt to politicize the gospel. Unlike Christian leaders who use biblical knowledge to advance political agendas, Chad Hovind is politically aware but biblically motivated. The Kingdom-first approach is evident."

—Jerry Robinson, economist, author of *Bankruptcy of Our Nation*,
and radio host of *Follow the Money (FTM)*

GODONOMICS

How to Save Our Country
—and Protect Your Wallet—
Through Biblical Principles of Finance

CHAD HOVIND

MULTNOMAH
B O O K S

GODONOMICS
PUBLISHED BY MULTNOMAH BOOKS
12265 Oracle Boulevard, Suite 200
Colorado Springs, Colorado 80921

Hardcover ISBN: 978-1-60142-477-8
eBook ISBN: 978-1-60142-478-5

Published in the United States by WaterBrook Multnomah, an imprint of the Crown Publishing Group, a division of Random House Inc., New York.

MULTNOMAH and its mountain colophon are registered trademarks of Random House Inc.

Library of Congress Cataloging-in-Publication Data
Hovind, Chad.
    Godonomics : how to save our country-and protect your wallet-through biblical principles of finance / Chad Hovind. — First Edition.
        pages cm
    Includes bibliographical references.
    ISBN 978-1-60142-477-8 — ISBN 978-1-60142-478-5 (electronic)
  1. Economics in the Bible. 2. Capitalism—Biblical teaching. 3. Politics in the Bible. 4. Economics—Religious aspects—Christianity. 5. Capitalism—Religious aspects—Christianity. 6. Economics—United States. 7. Capitalism—United States. 8. Christianity and politics—United States. I. Title.
    BS670.H68 2013
    261.8'5—dc23

                                        2013009411

Printed in the United States of America
2013—First Edition

10 9 8 7 6 5 4 3 2 1

CONTENTS

PART 7: If God Were Talking to Karl Marx

PART 8: If God Were Talking to the Internal Revenue Service

PART 9: If God Were Talking to You and Me

PREFACE

For nearly twenty years I have pastored churches in a variety of settings—from the small town of Groveland, Illinois, where I grew up to the pastoral staff of Moody Memorial Church in downtown Chicago. I've been part of nondenominational church plants in Georgia and more recently in Cincinnati. Some of the churches where I ministered were homogenous, while others were multiracial. Some congregations were predominantly "blue state," while others were predominantly "red state." I have worked hard not to paint God, Jesus, and the Bible with a political overlay.

The congregation I pastor today is filled with people who hold a myriad of political positions—from strongly conservative to moderate to liberal minded. Like me, they have found that God's grace in the message of the Cross unifies people across racial, social, political, and economic lines. They have discovered the value and importance of discussing beliefs and issues, God's will for individuals and nations, and sharing views on the great challenges that face us as Christians and Americans. All of these concerns apply to us as we attempt to understand and apply the Bible's teachings to everyday life.

That doesn't mean there aren't differing opinions and disagreements among church members. But if you were to meet my church members, whether they reflect the views of management or labor, Democrat or Republican, black or white, you will find we enjoy the freedom to disagree agreeably. We treat one another with respect and openness, regardless of where each of us might land on the big issues.

And while we enjoy the give and take of discussions about faith, what it means to follow Jesus, and a Christian's responsibilities in a free society, we all agree that the Bible is authoritative in all matters. Though Scripture does not suggest a particular political program for implementing Jesus's command to "do unto others," it does provide clear principles that intersect and transcend culture. The Bible speaks to all areas of life: marriage, government, finances, freedom, life, civil rights, prosperity, economics, science, and history.

As I wrote *Godonomics,* I realized I was entering potentially divisive territory. I was entering the Bermuda Triangle of "no-no's," speaking about God, money, and politics all at the same time. I have tried to present both the absolutes and the clear implications of God's unchanging precepts. Political and economic systems change, but God and His Word never change. Meanwhile, writing a book about economics always has political implications, which can be inherently divisive. My hope is that *Godonomics* will create a new context to think, dialogue, and reason together as fellow Americans, rather than raise issues that will be used to demonize one another. By appealing to an impartial, historic standard to measure our opinions and commitments, I hope to create a tool for healthy and helpful discussion, not division.

That said, you will find that *Godonomics* encourages every Christ-follower to venture into the minefield of politics and to help influence our nation's economic system. My hope is that every follower of Christ will humbly examine the call to public service in local, state, and federal leadership. As I write these words, I acknowledge that as I wrote this book, I struggled with the fear that I would be labeled one of "those" pastors who mixes religion and politics. Worse than that, I wade in with both feet, discussing religion, politics, and money. However, it is necessary to do so. These subjects have been left without deep philosophical and biblical insight for too long. Not since the groundbreaking work of Francis Schaeffer has the biblical worldview been pushed boldly and strategically into the public forum.

I am not saying that other efforts have been ineffective or that I am the

next Francis Schaeffer. But I am a pastor who feels called to speak out on issues of personal and family finance as well as our nation's economy and
monetary policies. As I mentioned, it is impossible to do this without also
addressing political issues and the biblical principles and values that guided
our nation's founding, and doing so in a great variety of settings. These are
critical issues, and I am committed to speaking, writing, and providing other
resources that can help Americans understand our nation's spiritual heritage
and how our leaders have lost sight of much that made our nation stand out
in the world. (For more on this, go to www.godonomics.com.)

I am a follower of Christ and a student of history, science, philosophy,
and the Scriptures. I have walked with skeptics, seekers, and fellow Christians in discovering the Bible's historically reliable and life-changing message.
I have found the exclusive claims of Jesus Christ to be not only the narrow
path to eternal life but also the grounds for tolerance toward people of all
beliefs and in all walks of life. A paradox is found at the core of the Bible's
claims: truth and grace.

The Bible presents the truth about ourselves, life, the world, and God.
These claims occasionally overlap with other world philosophies and religions, but more often than not they stand apart. They present a unique,
countercultural vision and worldview that challenges every other value system. The teachings of the Bible challenge assumptions made by Greeks/Ro-
mans, Nietzsche/Freud, pharaohs/kings, Socrates/Plato, and the religious as
well as the irreligious.

The message of the gospel contradicts both the moralist view of the reli-
giously devoted and the immorality of the pagan. It challenges the hopeless-
ness of naturalism while inviting the agnostic to come and see. It humbles the
religious adherent who has found comfort in self-righteousness while offering
a way to exalt the outcast. It unveils a mind-blowing kaleidoscope into the
nature of God. He is revealed to be more loving, wise, just, beautiful, holy,
accepting, approachable, and powerful than anyone would imagine.

I hope *Godonomics* will challenge you to experience more productivity, more prosperity, and more generosity than ever before. By presenting clear evidence of our Founding Fathers' political rationale for establishing and governing a free society, I hope you will understand and appreciate anew your God-given rights. May the historic facts and biblical truth not only challenge your political theories but transcend them to clarify your political convictions.

You should know, before we begin, that the Bible is the source of what I believe and the basis for how I live. I want to reason with you from Scripture, history, evidence, and logic why our nation is now on the wrong track economically. At the same time, I want to introduce you to the Jesus you may never have experienced.

I am thankful for my congregation at Horizon Community Church for giving me a platform to dialogue with explorers and Christ-followers alike.

I am thankful for the trust given to me by the hundreds of attendees who come each week, open to being equipped, challenged, or persuaded.

I am so grateful for my wife of eighteen years, Beth Hovind. (Or is it nineteen years?) I am humbled that God has given us three wonderful children to love and laugh with: Sierra, Javan, and Quinn.

I am also thankful to Moody Bible Institute, where I pursued undergraduate and graduate work, and the Willow Creek Association, with whom I have pastored for the last twenty years.

I am also thankful for the video team at www.godonomics.com who turned the teaching of Godonomics into a six-session video curriculum for use in churches, small groups, patriotic events, schools, and even homeschool environments.

I am honored to work with a great creative team, led by Paul Tate, which creates and presents the most inspiring, challenging, and creative services each week.

Finally, I am thankful for our church elders, executive board, and staff, who work with me to create an irresistible environment every week to welcome both the convinced and the unconvinced.

What Does God Say About Economics?

What you don't know can hurt you. We ignore the power of ideas at our own peril. All ideas, right or wrong, have spiritual, practical, or economic consequences.

Economics is an inexact science at best. Economists draw from the study of mathematics, statistics and probability, past economic trends, and a guiding philosophy that a particular school of economic theory provides the brightest light to follow. It's a little like weather forecasting, except that meteorology doesn't affect your retirement by getting mixed up in political skirmishes and power struggles at the highest levels of government. Not to mention that a faulty weather forecast will never destroy your family's finances or blot out a secure economic future.

Don't dismiss these possibilities as things that happen only in other countries or to other people. You and your family, your friends and neighbors, and the country you love can all be caught in the aftermath of a financial hurricane if America continues on its irresponsible and unsustainable economic path.

Here is what our leaders in both major parties do not seem to understand: political solutions can never put us on a sound economic footing. Politics is not interested primarily in the good of the nation. Instead, politics has to do with gaining and exercising power over your opponents, rewarding your biggest donors, and benefitting the priority constituencies of your party. If, in doing these things, you also accomplish something that is good for the country at large, that's great. But such an outcome is more an afterthought in the political process than it is a primary focus.

That might sound cynical, but if you fear I have cast my lot with the naysayers rather than choosing to work for a solution, keep reading. Recognizing why things are not working is the first step toward correcting the things that have gone terribly wrong.

The problem is that our nation's leaders look to deals and compromise to determine policy and enact legislation, and they are guided by political and economic ideologies that shape their values and priorities. They need, instead, the guidance of a fixed standard and a voice that speaks outside of our time and culture. In a world filled with donkeys, elephants, and rhinos, we need a lion that can roar timeless, common-sense principles that are not beholden to any party, time period, or cultural shift.

What our nation's leaders have missed is the one reliable, unfailing source of direction and wisdom that is available to us. If we continue to ignore God's guidance in the economic realm—at the levels of individuals, families, and the nation—we can be sure we'll end up losing even more of our freedom and personal wealth. We will be living in a country weakened by economic failure and wondering how the greatest nation in history could have been brought to such a depressing state of financial and ethical bankruptcy.

But that doesn't have to happen. The voice of the people can still carry the day. I am not suggesting a new Reformation that takes on a political identity. Nor am I calling for a theocracy in which Americans would be required to adhere to the doctrines of Christianity. In our republic, the voice and will of a majority of the citizens still possess the power to move our nation in a different direction—if we are united.

Why Godonomics?

What is Godonomics, and why is it the best way to solve the deepening economic dilemma we face as a nation, as families, and as individuals? Godonomics is, as the name suggests, God's teachings and wisdom in the realm of finance and economics. When you study the Bible, you find that God's agenda for nations, families, and individuals is not hard to understand. But it is not easy to apply, either. It requires commitment, restraint, godly priorities, hard work, and generosity, among other virtues. These words are not used a lot in political campaigns, because candidates for office prefer to paint their policies in terms of solutions that won't require hardship, sacrifice, or major shifts in priorities. God, of course, is not swayed by the results of opinion polls or the planks in a party platform.

And here is what is so refreshing in the principles of Godonomics: they make perfect sense. Speaking to us today through the scribes who recorded God's message over millenniums, God's plan for economic sanity, financial responsibility, and prosperity apply directly to the mess we are in today. Americans need to know that the options are not limited to Democratic, Republican, Libertarian, Socialist, Tea Party, and all other groups working to gain influence and power. While each one claims to have the secret to solving our broken economy, only God's principles will lead us out of the quagmire we're in. I believe that when Godonomics becomes widely known, and more and more people begin to apply God's principles at home, in their businesses, and in their communities, they will see for themselves that this is the solution we've been looking for.

Today's failed economic policies are nothing new. In the chapters that follow, we will look at ancient kings who seem to have taken their cues straight from John Maynard Keynes—except that Keynes would not be born for another three thousand years. We will look at the words and thinking of God-inspired leaders from Israel who recorded wisdom on leadership, government, citizenship, and personal responsibility—all of which helped guide the founders of the United States as they created our nation's legal and constitutional foundation. The same ancient wisdom undergirded the economic system that helped establish America as the most secure and prosperous country on earth.

Beyond that, the first Christ-followers applied these principles as individuals and families, and in congregations and fellowships. God's instructions are not vague or hard to understand. They simply require single-mindedness, hard work, generosity, and steadfast commitment. But following His instructions brings unmatched freedom, opportunity, and self-directed prosperity.

Godonomics seeks to bring God's economic principles to the forefront, so we can set our lives, our families' futures, and our nation on a sound financial footing—now and for the future. But there is a second—even more important—reason why Godonomics is so crucial. A rapidly growing movement has lured believers away from God's principles on finances and convinced them that socialism is, according to Scripture, the economic system that is most consistent with God's will.

Younger Christians, especially, are intrigued by persuasive Christian authors, speakers, and bloggers who emphasize giving priority to helping the poor by taking from others or empowering intrusive governments. They use the term *social justice* to advocate a shift of the economic balance in favor of those who are not producing wealth. They justify this stance with verses from the Bible, primarily from the Sermon on the Mount, the book of Acts, or selections from the Old Testament, without seeing the broader contexts. Growing numbers of younger Christians, who are largely unaware of the divine wisdom behind Godonomics, now consider socialism to be the economic system that God endorses. Advocates of this teaching do not call it socialism, of course. They use words such as *compassion, justice,* even *gospel,* to legitimize their goal of shifting wealth away from those who are productive and creating opportunities for others, and toward those who are said to be disadvantaged and marginalized.

I have pastored inner-city congregations that aggressively addressed the challenge and harm of generational poverty. I also have pastored suburban churches that are insulated from the plight of starving neighbors. I've been humbled to lead people from a variety of perspectives: One church was racially diverse while others were lily white. Some congregations were predominantly "blue state," while others were much more politically conservative. I've learned that people of all backgrounds and perspectives love our country, have a common-sense approach to life, and are not nearly as divided personally as the leaders they elect portray.

It is time for Christians and all Americans to join together to protect our heritage and to restore strength, stability, and prosperity to our nation. At the same time, it is essential that this be done from the bottom up, generated by individuals and families who take seriously God's wisdom on managing and stewarding their finances. Change will begin to take place only when citizens—both Christian and otherwise—act on the framework and guidelines upon which our nation was built. That is when we will see families prosper and our nation regain economic strength.

In the chapters that follow, we will look at the ideas and outcomes of leading thinkers and practitioners. We will examine policies based on economic theories that produced wealth and elevated the standard of living across the board, as well as those that weakened capitalism and, as a result, our nation. We will take a close look at capitalism's most influential foe, Karl Marx, and the current American spokesman for the rechristened social gospel, Jim Wallis, head of Sojourners.

There is nothing more personal than your next paycheck, your financial future, and your family's freedom, security, and well-being. So let's see what God would say if He were talking individually to the economic thinkers and political leaders who shape and enact the policies that govern our country. These are the policies that have an impact in your town, in your home, and on your wallet. Let's get started.

PART 1

If God Were Talking to America's Founders

It Is No Accident That God Endorses Capitalism

All economic systems are not equal

In the earliest days of what became the Massachusetts Bay Colony, a group we know as the Pilgrims landed on Cape Cod and established a settlement. They were not wearing belt buckles on their hats, but it is true that they came to the New World with the dream of finding liberty and prosperity by building a new way of life. Governor William Bradford's group adopted a charter requiring them to practice communal living, or socialism. It sounded like a great concept. Everyone would work for the common good by farming the land together and sharing their produce equally.

They were religious and moral people, so their experiment in centralized economics seemed godly, sensible, and relatively easy to implement. Why wouldn't this devoted group take part energetically in the labor as well as share freely the products of their labor? Well, it looked good on paper.

The first months were devastating. Many of the colonists were seemingly too busy to work the fields. Others didn't feel physically able to work and assumed that others would make up for their absence. In the first year, an alarming 50 percent of the Pilgrims who settled at Plymouth died from starvation. Harsh weather worked against them, but a second devastating condition was something they could have avoided. Their stores of food were insufficient to keep the entire colony healthy and well fed. Too many of the available workers failed to do their part, so not enough food was grown to feed the colony.

Bradford tried to rally the group with a stirring reminder that if they did not join together to get the necessary work done, more people would die. One year later, hundreds more perished. Again, too many had chosen not to do their part. Could it be that the first New World experiment in socialism was so misguided that lives were lost as a result? How could immigrants who had found a place where they could practice their faith according to their consciences allow such a deadly outcome when they had the power to prevent it?

Property Rights, Incentive, Freedom

Bradford decided to search the Scriptures and seek insight from God. He found three principles that saved the village and possibly even the great nation that would follow. The foundational principles were property rights, incentive, and freedom. In the Bible, he discovered a blueprint for a new economic system.

Throughout Scripture we see clear guidance on finances. When God brought His people out of Egypt and taught them to live in a new land as free people, He gave them ten building blocks for society. Among the Ten Commandments, God said, "Do not covet or steal someone else's house or donkey..." (see Exodus 20:15, 17). Laws against envy and theft make it clear that God honors an individual's right of ownership. By God's decree, each person would have ownership of his or her personal belongings, such as cattle and land. Bradford noted that the concept of property rights appeared throughout the Scripture, including Acts 5:1–4, where Ananias's field was his own to dispose of as he pleased.

On the second foundational principle, incentive, Bradford was surprised that the Scriptures spoke so decisively: "If anyone will not work, neither shall he eat" (2 Thessalonians 3:10); "Give her [the virtuous wife] of the fruit of her hands" (Proverbs 31:31); "You shall not muzzle an ox while it treads out the grain" (Deuteronomy 25:4).[1]

Bradford called a town meeting and notified the colonists they would no longer operate according to the old model. It had allowed shirkers to share in the produce that came from the labor of others. The unforeseen, disastrous outcome was that the workers who had done their part were unable to produce enough food to feed the entire community. In place of their early experiment in socialism, Bradford implemented the basics of capitalism by giving families the freedom to work their own land to grow their own food and to produce any other goods as they saw fit. There was no central economic authority assigning duties or managing details of production. It was up to each family to determine how they would utilize their property and resources to provide for their needs.

Bradford formulated the colony's new economic system based on the three principles that God had given the Hebrews: property rights, incentive, and personal freedom.

With work now being conducted under the rules of the new system, something amazing happened. Husbands and wives, children and relatives, all worked together on their own farms. Each person and family had incentive to work hard to provide for themselves and those they felt responsible for.

The result was a bumper crop. There was such a large harvest that families had food for themselves and plenty left over to share with others. Thus, they celebrated the first Thanksgiving with turkey feasts and thanked God for His provision and wisdom. Bradford wrote about this experiment in his journal, warning future generations that socialism doesn't work. Collectivism may sound like the perfect answer for right-thinking people, but the results in the Massachusetts Bay Colony were devastating.[2] If socialism didn't work in this best-case scenario with devout Christians, why would we think a less-than-ideal paradigm would work? In other words, if a mostly devout Christian community in the past couldn't make it work, is there any hope Washington, DC, will get it right today?

God's economic principles of property rights, incentive, and personal freedom are central to what I refer to as Godonomics. The value of this economic system was not limited to the ancient Hebrews when they were headed to their new homeland in Canaan. And the effectiveness of this system did not end with America's earliest European immigrants. Personal freedom, incentive, and property rights are universal principles, serving as the bedrock of a free-market economy. In later chapters we'll discuss the first two. For now, let's take a closer look at property rights.

Property Rights

Property rights are referred to in two of the Ten Commandments. We are warned not to envy someone else's house or horse—wishing that something belonging to another person was ours (see Exodus 20:17). Another commandment, "You shall not steal," is a direct statement that because ownership is specific to a person, you have no right to appropriate what does not belong to you (Exodus 20:15).

God respects a person's right to ownership so much that He forbids our even wanting to own what belongs to another. Beyond that, actually taking what does not belong to you is a legal issue. Why should you or I avoid taking something that is not ours? Because God has established that someone else owns the rights to that asset. For the Hebrews, this law meant that no longer would a "Pharaoh" own the land they worked and lived on as they moved into their new land and future together. They, not the community or leader, would *individually* own property. No longer would the strongest and most powerful militia determine who owns and controls the resources and wealth on the basis of survival of the wickedest.

Property rights serve as the key contrast between socialism and capitalism. There is confusion today among Americans as to the meaning of these words and the economic system each represents. For example, a person might characterize capitalism as a system that relies on greed to drive economic success and socialism as the system that emphasizes generosity by caring for the disadvantaged. But when each system is exercised in society, the results reveal the exact opposite.

Here are working definitions of the two major economic systems:

- *Capitalism:* the free exchange of privately owned goods and services
- *Socialism:* state control and state ownership of industry and property

Private ownership of property ensures personal freedom (another foundational principle of a free-market economy) because it emphasizes that the individual is more important than the state. Was Spock correct in *Star Trek II: The Wrath of Khan* when he said, "Logic clearly dictates that the needs of the many outweigh the needs of the few?"[3] Does the Borg's collectivism justify assimilation of the individual? According to God, the answer is no.

C. S. Lewis provided a clear summation of the biblical worldview:

Christianity asserts that every individual human being is going to live forever, and this must be either true or false.... If individuals live only seventy years, then a state, or a nation, or a civilization, which may last for a thousand years, is more important than an individual. But if Christianity is true, then the individual is not only more important but incomparably more important, for he is everlasting and the life of the state or civilization, compared with his, is only a moment.[4]

The difference between socialism and free-market capitalism is massive. Socialism believes the individual should serve the state. But the Bible is clear that, in a free society, the state is the protector of an individual's rights. The two perspectives are diametrically opposed.

If God gave rights to individuals at the creation of humanity, then individuals hold the power. They might choose to loan certain rights to the state for select purposes. For example, individuals might want their local community to employ firefighters and law-enforcement personnel. To make that possible, they would vote for a reasonable tax levy. In return, the local government protects citizens and their property against the danger of fire and enforces laws.

However, if rights are held by the state, then rights are arbitrary. They can be granted or withdrawn at the determination of the state. The state might decide that to ensure the greater good, certain rights need to be restricted. Such a statist system is foreign to the teachings of the Bible.

The state cannot grant rights to individuals, since our rights are God-given and hard-wired into us. The role of the state is to *protect* God-given rights. When the state attempts to overrule God's role as the Grantor of rights, it is putting itself in the place of God, which is evil. This is one reason why socialism is a failed economic system. It is also the reason why God opposes socialism and advances the foundations on which capitalism is based.

God could give us the principles for any economic system imaginable. Remember our working definitions of capitalism and socialism:

- *Capitalism:* the free exchange of privately owned goods and services
- *Socialism:* state control and state ownership of industry and property

God chose to endorse the building blocks of capitalism thousands of years before it was given that label. Remember that since God owns everything, He could have chosen to grant temporary, earthly ownership to the state rather than to individuals. But based on His perfect knowledge of the future and knowing how societies work best for the benefit of the people, God chose to place rights in the hands of the individual. So why, today, is there such a vocal movement favoring the shift of rights away from citizens so power can be concentrated in the state? How presumptuous is it for humans to advance a method that God—the only One qualified for the job—rejected from the beginning?

Christians and some others who are concerned about returning America to its founding principles are rediscovering the biblical basis for freedom and economic strength and opportunity. This makes Godonomics a crucial study for us as we move deeper into uncertain times with ongoing economic challenges that none of us have faced before.

Godonomics is the power of God's wisdom applied to a personal, family, and even national economy. It is the blueprint and framework for achieving and enjoying liberty, prosperity, and generosity. And frankly, Godonomics is something that used to be called common sense.

To help us begin our exploration of economic systems, as well as personal and family finance, let's look back to the eighteenth century and a philosopher who had keen insight into God's wisdom as applied to capitalism.

PART 2

If God Were Talking to Philosopher Adam Smith

What Would God Say to Adam Smith About Work?

How capitalism elevates the importance of work

The identification of three biblical principles that lay the foundation of capitalism is not a recent development. As early as 1776, Christian moral philosopher Adam Smith wrote extensively about the biblical basis for a successful society. At the University of Glasgow, he wrote a book titled *The Wealth of Nations*. His thinking as expressed in that book provided the philosophical foundation and launch pad for modern capitalism. Not only were his ideas freeing, since they argued against centralized control of economic choices, but they advanced the one economic system that proved its validity by launching a worldwide revolution in prosperity.

Consider just two realities of life in Western Europe prior to the widespread adoption of Smith's principles:

- Prior to 1780, four-fifths of French citizens expended 90 percent of their income on food.
- As recently as 1780 in Germany, fewer than a thousand people earned more than a thousand dollars annually.[1]

However, as religious leaders and others began to advance Smith's thinking as it applied to economics and liberty, it was not long before a wave of prosperity was unleashed.

- From 1800 to 1850, wages quadrupled.
- From 1850 to 1900, wages quadrupled again.

- During the nineteenth century in England, actual wealth and income increased sixteen times over. In America, the results were even more impressive.[2]

Smith is known as the Father of Modern Economics. Following is a modern parable that illustrates his basic approach, showing why it has been so successful in producing prosperity and economic stability.

An economics teacher was trying to convince his class that capitalism fueled incentive while socialism did not. He wanted students to understand that capitalism, as a system, produced benefits for society, while socialism—as expressed in Marxism—could not avoid penalizing the citizens of any society. Since the students had been influenced by communistic thinking, the teacher devised a practical way to bring socialism home.

When the time came for the first written test of the semester, the teacher graded the papers and gave every student a C+. The students protested, of course. Those who had studied hard argued that they had earned an A. (Others kept quiet, because they had not bothered to study and were happy to receive a C+.) But the teacher justified the across-the-board granting of the same grade on the basis that he was treating everyone equally, just as a socialistic system required. By averaging the efforts of the class, he had arrived at a C+.

The experiment produced an immediate effect. On the next test, the A-level students didn't bother to study. The slackers simply continued their poor study habits, since doing nothing had already landed them a C+. However, with less effort now being expended by the entire class, the average on the second test fell to a D.

The students began to catch on. Treating everyone equally leads to a drop in motivation and results in diminished achievement. It robs hard workers of the fruit of their hard work. And it unfairly rewards laziness and apathy, "paying" the do-nothings the same wage, so to speak, as the top producers.[3]

Capitalism delivers benefits that go far beyond the three foundational pillars of property rights, incentive, and personal freedom. Capitalism is a channel for two gifts that lead to personal and national prosperity: the gift of work and the gift of profit. The gift of profit will be covered in the next chapter.

The Gift of Work

At the heart of Godonomics is the value of work and the God-given joy that comes with it. Labor is a gift to us from God. He gave each of us talents to develop and opportunities in which to apply our talents. God wants His people to work in order to provide for themselves and others, rather than depending on others to supply what we need to survive. This principle dates back to the beginning. As soon as God created humanity, He gave the first couple work to do.

"Then the LORD God took the man and put him in the garden of Eden to tend and keep it" (Genesis 2:15).

It is critical that we see work as important and recognize it as a biblical command. The Scriptures teach that all of life is spiritual. Work can be as holy as prayer or taking communion, since all of life should be approached as an act of service to God.

This concept of life in its entirety being a spiritual endeavor was advanced by Paul in his New Testament writings (see Romans 12:1–2; Colossians 3:23–24). Paul's unified approach—joining one's earthly life with one's service to God—offers us a radically different lens through which to view and understand our existence, meaning, and purpose. This stands in stark contrast to the prevailing dualistic philosophy of Paul's day (the first century).

Dualism, also known as Gnosticism, is the belief that spiritual activities are distinct and separate from so-called nonspiritual activities, which include the ordinary tasks of everyday living.

The Bible teaches that every moment of every day is to be infused with the potential of pleasing God. There is no distinction between spiritual and nonspiritual. Whether you like your job or not. Whether you get along with your boss or not. The Bible says work is far more than simply a means to obtaining a paycheck. When we arrive at work every day, we ultimately are working for God. When we use every moment as a spiritual act of worship (see Romans 12:1–2), we are looking forward to enjoying a reward for our labor that goes far beyond an automatic payroll deposit. There is both an earthly reward (a paycheck and growing savings) and a heavenly reward. Each of us wants to hear "Well done, good servant" (Luke 19:17). God will reward you eternally for working diligently and wisely in this life.

Adam Smith recognized not only the necessity of work but also its goodness. His book *Wealth of Nations* was a sequel to the earlier work *The Theory of Moral Sentiments,* in which he taught the importance of having a morally educated society. Smith spoke of both self-love, which he defined as the desire to work and be productive, and self-command, an inward honing of the Golden Rule. We gain mastery over ourselves by practicing a life of acting toward others as we desire others to act toward us. Smith considered these two motivations—self-love and self-command—to be the foundation of a moral free-enterprise system. He wrote, "Self-command is not only itself a great virtue, but from it all the other virtues seem to derive their principal lustre."[4]

All Work Is Done for God

All work is done ultimately for God, which is a primary motivation of self-command. God is the ultimate Spectator and Rewarder. Adam Smith described the marriage of moral training and self-interest, which undergird a free society and free-market capitalism:

> There can be no proper motive for hurting our neighbor.… To disturb
> his happiness merely because it stands in the way of our own, to take
> from him what is of real use to him merely because it may be of equal
> or of more use to us,…is what no impartial spectator can go along
> with.… In the race for wealth, and honours, and preferments, he may
> run as hard as he can, and strain every nerve and every muscle, in
> order to outstrip all his competitors. But if he should justle [sic], or
> throw down any of them, the indulgence of the spectators is entirely at
> an end. It is a violation of fair play, which they cannot admit of.[5]

The apostle Paul developed a comprehensive applied theology of work. "And whatever you do, do it heartily, as to the Lord and not to men, knowing that from the Lord you will receive the reward of the inheritance; for you serve the Lord Christ" (Colossians 3:23–24).

A Christ-follower is not working primarily for an earthly employer. God watches our work and adds the incentive of reward. "You will receive the reward of the inheritance" (Colossians 3:24). We will receive a reward as we stand before God and He lavishes us with gifts at the judgment seat of Christ. Those gifts will include greater responsibilities of service in His Heavenly Kingdom as well as deeper intimacy with God in eternity.

Jesus took these teachings even further. He said, "Inasmuch as you did it to one of the least of these My brethren, you did it to Me" (Matthew 25:40). Serving your clients, your boss, and your employees is a way to serve Christ Himself.

A commitment to hard work and productivity, and rewarding those who produce results, has been called "the Protestant work ethic." It is not limited to one segment of Christianity. It is, in fact, the mark of Christ-followers who live out the gift of work. Critics of capitalism argue that an economic system that is built on work, incentive, and reward too easily leads to workers hoarding the reward. But Jesus was careful to extend the benefits of Godonomics to those who genuinely need assistance. He pointed out that anyone who extended help to the "least of these" was doing it for Him personally. This teaching inspired a world-changing wave of generosity that continues to this day. Followers of Christ have used their talents in work, they have profited from their efforts, and they have given away a significant portion of their wealth. Their motivation has been simple: giving to the poor, hurting, widowed, imprisoned, and orphaned is a gift to God Himself.

In his book *What If Jesus Had Never Been Born?*, Dr. D. James Kennedy noted that even Fidel Castro had seen the benefits of this mind-set. "Fidel Castro has on occasion reluctantly admitted that he admires many of the evangelicals in Cuba," Kennedy wrote. "This is because they are hard workers; they show up to work on time; they don't cheat the system."[6]

Thus, even a Communist dictator had recognized the practical benefits of a biblical work ethic.

But adding a veneer of Christianity to one's business is not a guarantee that the goods and services will reflect a biblical approach. One friend who is not a follower of Christ told me that when he needs to hire a contractor, he looks first for the Christian fish symbol in advertisements in the Yellow Pages. I asked why, and he said, "The Christian fish means you are about to be ripped off. Don't use them!" To back up his claim, he told me story after story of being cheated by Christians.

Too often, people who claim to follow Christ are lazy, deceitful, or larcenous. They make excuses for their habit of cutting corners by blaming the company or their supervisor. They think God's grace is an excuse for mediocre efforts and wishy-washy commitments. Corporate policies are said to be too restrictive, or work requirements are seen as too demanding and unrealistic. But the bottom line is such workers are not working in the way God instructs. God commands us to bring a high level of excellence, commitment, and passion to every project as a way of honoring Him.

Taking Personal Responsibility

God says that instead of depending on others, we should bear our own load (see Galatians 6:5). Sadly, we are beginning to live in a society that produces people who have few marketable skills, little self-discipline, and not enough drive and ambition to compete successfully in the marketplace. People are handicapped financially, emotionally, and spiritually when they are constantly rescued from difficulty. In the physical realm, someone who never exercises their muscles will never develop more strength and agility. And in all of life, people can't become strong and proficient unless they carry their own load. We must work toward financial independence as God supplies our needs rather than being a burden on others.

Paul introduced the Christian concepts of examining one's work and bearing one's own load into a Greek and Roman culture where aristocrats didn't do manual labor. That attitude spread to the majority of citizens, who considered work to be the responsibility of servants. Paul mentioned having visited Athens, where he noted that the aristocrats spent their time in frivolous pastimes. Luke describes it this way: "For all the Athenians and the foreigners who were there spent their time in nothing else but either to tell or to hear some new thing" (Acts 17:21). Philosophizing and pondering are a far cry from working and producing.

The Greek philosophy of Gnosticism taught that the unknowable god was far too pure to have anything to do with the material universe. They considered matter inherently evil, and this mind-set kept people from cherishing the work that was required to produce crops for food and goods for the marketplace.

The message of Christianity was radically different, however. God took on matter in the person of Jesus Christ. Therefore, matter could not be inherently evil. The incarnation of God the Son in Jesus teaches us that matter matters. The material world can and should be used for good. Cultivating and working in the physical world is a powerful way to imitate our Creator, and the early Christians understood this.

Paul issued a direct challenge to Gnosticism by teaching that work is a gift, a calling, and a command from God. Self-sufficiency is a way to not be a burden on others. At the same time, working toward self-sufficiency fans into flame the talents and potential deposited in each of us by a loving Creator. Paul wrote, "But let each one examine his own work, and then he will have rejoicing in himself alone, and not in another. For each one shall bear his own load" (Galatians 6:4–5).

When a person is lazy but a community or society at large provides for her needs, the slothful individual assumes that laziness should be rewarded. In God's economy, work is rewarded while sloth is condemned. In a family setting, if teenagers have enjoyed an easy life with Mom and Dad, it can be hard to launch them into the work force. They have learned that it's possible to live comfortably without carrying their own load. If parents fail to prepare their children to take responsibility for their own lives, the next generation will never learn to become independent, productive adults.

I talk to employers from different fields who say they have trouble finding college graduates who do not have an entitlement attitude. Such an attitude minimizes a person's ability to work hard, work honestly, and work with excellence. Employers are looking for people who embody these qualities—who work when they are not being watched. Companies need employees who go the extra mile to help build a successful business, rather than just take home a paycheck. They want people who treat their bosses the way they want to be treated—with respect rather than contempt, grace rather than insubordination.

Employees seek similar things. They want bosses to pay a fair salary or wage, to reward hard work, and to create an environment of respect.

The Role of Generosity

Christ-followers have a dual responsibility. Each person is responsible for carrying his or her own load, as we saw in Galatians 6:4–5. At the same time, each one needs to be looking for ways to help those who have a legitimate need or "burden": "Bear one another's burdens, and so fulfill the law of Christ" (verse 2). Paul's choice of words is important. You are to carry your own "load" and carry other people's "burdens." The distinction between the two is critical.

A woman came to me for advice after her brother, a man in his fifties, had asked her again for money to pay his bills. He had lost his money in gambling. She had already bailed him out several times over the past twenty years.

I asked why she kept helping a man who clearly needed to face the consequences of his irresponsible actions. She said that their mother had bailed him out for years. The brother had lived with their mother, using guilt to manipulate her into covering his financial losses. The man's sister told me that she, as well, felt like she had to help her brother.

"But why?" I asked. She told me that her mother, on her deathbed, had made her promise that she would keep helping him. This woman now felt angry about being taken advantage of. At the same time, she knew that Jesus commanded His followers to help "the least of these."

Paul's teachings in Galatians speak directly to this woman's struggle. She needed to know that the command to carry your own load applied to her brother, who needed to take responsibility for his own finances. The principles of Godonomics give this woman the freedom to help out if she sees her brother moving steadily toward health, responsibility, and ownership of his problem. At the same time, her brother needs to experience the consequences of his unwise choices and his years-long habit of exploiting others. Suffering the consequences of your flawed choices is consistent with the New Testament principle of sowing and reaping (see Galatians 6:7).

The Bible gives us two ways to determine the difference between your own load and another person's burden.

Loads vs. Burdens

A "burden" is a crushing weight, something that goes far beyond a "load," which is a responsibility you can handle on your own. In contrast, a burden might be an out-of-control emotional struggle, an overwhelming physical challenge, or a financial reversal that threatens to undo everything an individual and his or her family rely on for survival. When others are crushed by such a burden, a follower of Christ must come to their aid. This is how we fulfill the law of Christ (see Galatians 6:2).

Jewish historian Josephus noted that the early church was so generous and sacrificial with its money that it came to the attention of Julian, the pagan emperor of Rome. Julian noted that because "the impious Galilaeans support not only their own poor but ours as well, all men see that our people lack aid from us."[7]

The abundance of Christian generosity was quite a contrast in a Roman world where no one gave anything to anyone.

As we help someone, we have to assess the need as well as the effect of our help. We help with the person's crushing "burden" but leave it to them to carry their own "load." No one wants to be put in a position of dependency. Doing our fair share is part of our innate sense of right and wrong, even among children. How many times have you told your children to clean the family room, then after they've been in there awhile, one of them announces, "I did more than him! He's not pulling his weight!"

Self-Centeredness vs. Self-Interest

When you carry your own load, not only are you taking responsibility for your life, you are making sure that your own best interests do not get overlooked. No one else is as interested in your welfare and the well-being of your family as you are. So it makes sense that you will apply yourself to work and do what is needed to be productive. Work is designed, in part, to secure the financial resources to meet the basic needs of your family. Often, it also makes possible opportunities for family members to grow socially, intellectually, in the arts, and so forth.

Maximizing your productivity to provide for your own and your family's needs is a primary result of self-interest. In *The Wealth of Nations,* Adam Smith expounded on the importance of self-interest, the natural desire of any person to work to obtain the things that are necessary for survival, plus the things that add comfort, security, and enjoyment to life. When people pursue self-sufficiency, it supplies what their own families need—and also extends to helping ensure the good of society. Self-interested competition in a free market, Smith argued, benefits society as a whole by keeping prices low while expanding markets and by building an incentive for tradesmen, entrepreneurs, and merchants to provide a wider variety of goods and services. He wrote,

> It is not from the benevolence of the butcher, the brewer, or the baker, that we expect our dinner, but from their regard to their own interest. We address ourselves, not to their humanity but to their self-love, and never talk to them of our own necessities but of their advantages.[8]

How does this understanding of self-interest differ from self-centeredness, which is condemned in the Bible? If you depend on someone else to provide for you when you are capable of working, then you are selfish. You are benefitting from someone else's labor when you should be laboring yourself. That is self-centered behavior. The Bible admonishes the sluggard to wise up by studying the ant because the ant works hard, provides for its own needs, and builds savings for the future (see Proverbs 6:6–8).

Self-interest, in contrast, motivates personal responsibility and hard work by promising a fair reward to the worker. Self-interest gives craftsmen a reason to produce better products and to offer them for sale at a fair price, representing clear value to their customers. Thus, customers are able to purchase better products, and craftsmen now have an even greater incentive to expand their businesses, maximize their productivity, and enjoy greater rewards from their work.

According to biblical psychology, self-sufficiency is what motivates human planning and behavior. People are hard wired to look out for themselves. It is a theme throughout the Old and New Testaments. Jesus told us the greatest commandment is "Love the Lord your God" and the second greatest is "Love your neighbor as yourself" (Matthew 22:37–39; compare Deuteronomy 6:5; Leviticus 19:18). Notice that Jesus assumes that we love ourselves. We look out for ourselves. We protect ourselves. We provide for ourselves. We are motivated by self-interest.

Jesus uses the same logic with the Golden Rule: "Do to others as you would have them do to you" (Luke 6:31, NIV). Jesus assumed that we are well versed in the ways we want to be loved and provided for. He petitions us to use the moral law that is already written on our hearts as a guide for how we treat others. God's moral law written on every person's heart is one aspect of the grace God gives to all of us to help us function in a broken world (see Romans 2:15). In fact, the Puritans called this idea "common grace." Common grace is the basic understanding of right and wrong that God has given to humanity. Self-interest is an example of common grace; it guides us in doing the right thing.

Still, Paul taught that our self-interest is permeated with selfishness. Our hearts are fundamentally cracked, unable to consistently follow God's will. Though we are appropriately motivated by self-interest, we must be careful not to think only of our own needs. In Philippians, Paul put this in perspective: "Each of you should look not only to your own interests, but also to the interests of others" (Philippians 2:4, NIV).

Like Jesus, Paul assumes that we are looking out for our own interests.

Jesus said, in effect, love yourself and love others. Paul echoes that with "Look out for your interests *and* apply that natural instinct to looking out for others."

Free-market capitalism taps into this type of self-interest while also requiring people to put others' needs first in order to meet their own needs. A craftsman cannot sell his wares unless someone needs the items he produces. A family needs chairs to sit in, and they buy them from a furniture maker. Both the seller and buyer benefit from the transaction. The seller wants to make money but must offer a product at a price and quality that is attractive to the buyer. By placing the buyer's needs first, the seller is able to meet his own needs as well. Self-interest drives the seller's desire to profit and results in blessing others in a free-market society.

Just as there is a clear difference between the gift of profit and the decay of greed, there is a big difference between self-interest, which leads to beneficial profit, and selfishness, which fuels greed. Economist Milton Friedman addressed the difference in answer to questions from former talk-show host Phil Donahue. Friedman also pointed out the fallacies and dangers of socialistic societies.

DONAHUE: "When you see around the globe, the mal-distribution of wealth, the desperate plight of millions of people in underdeveloped countries,...don't you ever have a moment of doubt about capitalism? And whether greed's a good idea to run on?"

FRIEDMAN: "Well, first of all, tell me. Is there some society you know that doesn't run on greed? You think Russia doesn't run on greed? You think China doesn't run on greed? What is greed? Of course, none of us are greedy, it's only the other fella who's greedy. The world runs on individuals pursuing their self-interests. The great achievements of civilization have not come from government bureaus. Einstein didn't construct his theory under order from a bureaucrat. Henry Ford didn't revolutionize the automobile industry that way. In the only cases in which the masses have escaped from the kind of grinding poverty you're talking about, the only cases in recorded history are where they have had capitalism and largely free trade. If you want to know where the masses are worst off, it's exactly in the kinds of societies that depart from that. So that the record of history is absolutely crystal clear that there is no alternative way, so far discovered, of improving the lot of the ordinary people that can hold a candle to the productive activities that are unleashed by the free-enterprise system."[9]

The Bible teaches that although humans are marked by the fingerprint of God, the human heart is malformed. Any system of economics or politics must take humanity's sinful nature into consideration. This is why America's founders tried to minimize centralized governmental authority. To guard against abuse, they instituted checks and balances and distributed power in a number of important ways. They knew that throughout history, societies known for the most horrific greed, corruption, and centralized control were ruled by dictators, pharaohs, or kings who took wealth away from citizens in order to enrich those in power. Such a system has existed throughout history, long before the word *socialism* came into common use. Socialist, communist, and Marxist systems enable the elite to profit by exploiting the masses.

However, greed is minimized when commerce and production are freed from the control of a centralized governmental authority. As we have seen, a free-market economy trains workers and producers to focus on others. In a free-market system, you profit only when you are meeting the needs of others. This is one reason why Adam Smith supported a free market. He knew the biblical truth that all humans are sinful—consumers, politicians, business owners, workers, bankers, and leaders in government. One way to mitigate everyone's greed is by making sure there isn't one centralized power structure stealing from one group to benefit another group.

Smith had this to say:

> The natural effort of every individual to better his own condition, when suffered to exert itself with freedom and security is so powerful a principle that it is alone, and without any assistance, not only capable of carrying on the society to wealth and prosperity, but of surmounting a hundred impertinent obstructions with which the folly of human laws too often incumbers its operations. [10]

Smith was showing that—even in his day—the drive for increased government regulation resulted in waste, inefficiency, higher unemployment, and loss of personal liberty.

When a centrally controlled government regulates business, it does not reward hard work, but rather rewards political constituents and restrains political enemies. Smith notes that self-interest and free enterprise do reward personal initiative, hard work, and self-reliance. Centuries earlier, Paul addressed work and self-sufficiency:

> For you yourselves know how you ought to follow our example. We were not idle when we were with you, nor did we eat anyone's food without paying for it. On the contrary, we worked night and day, laboring and toiling so that we would not be a burden to any of you. We did this, not because we do not have the right to such help, but in order to make ourselves a model for you to follow. For even when we were with you, we gave you this rule: "If a man will not work, he shall not eat."
>
> We hear that some among you are idle. They are not busy; they are busybodies. *Such people we command and urge in the Lord Jesus Christ to settle down and earn the bread they eat.* (2 Thessalonians 3:7–12, NIV)

Not only did Paul stress the importance of hard work, but he provided insight into another Godonomics principle: property rights. Paul reminded the Christians living in Thessalonica that, during a past visit, he and his companions had not eaten "anyone's food *without* paying for it." He was showing that it is necessary to respect the property rights of others.

Paul then moved from property rights to incentive. "If a man will not work [assuming he is capable of work], he shall not eat" (verse 10, NIV). That is a pretty strong incentive! Paul rebuked those who were leeching off others, calling them "busybodies." In place of that, he required everyone to "earn the bread" he eats. Work is both a gift from God and the engine that powers free enterprise.

What Would God Say to Adam Smith About Profit?

How profit making forces sellers to focus on others' needs

Two gifts—work and profit—promote liberty, prosperity, and generosity. God does not shun profit making. In fact, His economic principles make profit possible.

Adam Smith noted that the "invisible hand" of free markets will ultimately bless others. Business owners have to be others focused in order to turn a profit. Here is how Godonomics works.

A strong economy is fueled by production, and producing leads to profit. Profit covers our expenses and builds savings. Out of savings we spend, invest, and give to others.

From the start, a free-market economic system is others centered. You can't make a profit unless you provide a product or service that someone else wants. You must ask, "What do people need? What would help them?" The product must be priced so that people will choose to buy it. If the price is too high, customers will go somewhere else.

By offering needed goods and services at fair prices, a person realizes a profit. The profits allow the person to invest in more ventures, potentially creating more jobs and producing more savings. Additional savings allow the person to give even more to others in need and to spend money on needed goods and services provided by others.

This process is described in Proverbs 31, where God used a successful businesswoman as a case study. She considers others' needs as she "perceives that her merchandise is good" (verse 18). If she were the customer, she would buy this merchandise at the price she has determined. She has an eye toward profit as she offers merchandise for sale, as she buys a field, and as she works the field.

The Bible celebrates the woman's profits, noting that she is owed "the fruit of her hands" (verse 31), that fruit being the financial profit generated by her businesses. Unfortunately, listening today to many in the news media and even in the church, you might conclude that God thinks profit is a four-letter word.

Our businesswoman puts her profits to good use. "From her profits she plants a vineyard" (verse 16). She is able to employ more people, this time by hiring workers to tend a vineyard. Job growth occurs when someone produces and profits as a result. The profits enable the person to invest in another enterprise. The new company will need to hire workers.

What to Do with Profits

Something powerful happens when you produce and profit. My son Javan wanted an Xbox last Christmas. We already had a Nintendo DS and a Wii.

I told him I would not be buying him an Xbox. Further, he was not allowed to do an end-around by asking Grandma or Grandpa to do what I was not willing to do.

PRODUCING   PROFITING   SAVING

Javan now had a strong incentive to work. He asked about chores he could do, and then he raised the possibility of auditioning for television commercials. We had pursued some television work for him earlier that year, but he lost interest.

Armed with incentive, my son started doing more chores, and he got a role in a Japanese reenactment reality show. He worked all day taking directions from a camera crew. Ironically, the episode was about a kid who got a Wii for Christmas and was so excited he threw up on camera, making him a YouTube sensation. My son looked like the kid in the video. After a full day's work, he was paid two hundred dollars. He had produced. He had profited. He had accumulated some savings.

He still didn't have enough money to buy a new Xbox, so he got on Craigslist and found a used Xbox for sale in Indiana for less than two hundred dollars. It came with additional memory and three video games. We high-fived each other, made the phone call, and headed to Indiana.

As we approached the seller's house, I chuckled that an Indiana teenager was about to accept half the retail value of an Xbox in this transaction. But that boy was thrilled to be making money, while his mother stood in the background shaking her head. She had bought the game system for her son just the previous Christmas.

The contrast was striking. My son was learning the value of work and money. Her son was learning how to sell a valuable item at a deep discount, forfeiting much of the item's value. And since the Xbox had been a gift, he was learning how to profit without having had worked for it.

From the time our kids were seven, Beth and I have taught them to put their money into three jars. Ten percent goes into a giving jar, 10 percent goes into a saving jar, and they are allowed to spend the remaining 80 percent. This has allowed them to begin learning Godonomics at a young age. Already they are practicing lessons from the Proverbs 31 woman: producing, profiting, saving, and giving.

In his book *Who Really Cares,* Arthur Brooks investigated the root causes of generous giving. He uncovered catalysts for generosity, which include strong families, church attendance, earned income (as opposed to state-subsidized income), and the belief that individuals, not government, are the best source for charity. He concluded that conservative people of faith are far more generous than their counterparts, whom he described as self-identified irreligious people with moderate to liberal political leanings.[1]

The example of the businesswoman in Proverbs 31 teaches us more than the value of producing, profiting, saving, and giving. Her story also emphasizes God's recognition of the right to ownership of property. The writer reflects this in verse 31: "Give her the fruit of her hands."

The profit generated by her businesses belonged to her. Incentive and property rights are two of the linchpins of free-market capitalism. The potential to generate profit was the incentive for her hard work, and the resulting profit made it possible for her to be generous in giving.

This system works well because it is built on liberty, prosperity, and generosity. She works freely. She prospers freely. She gives freely.

Concentrate on Fairness, Not Equality

Fairness is a crucial catalyst in translating these principles into action. It can be stated in five words: Treat people fairly, not equally.

The word *equality* is used a lot in our society, but too many Americans are confused about its proper meaning and role in a capitalistic economy. What does "treating everyone equally" mean when it is put into practice?

My father taught me to juggle and to make figures out of balloons when I was a child. Now I am passing these skills on to my children, ages nine and twelve. It's both a fun hobby and a skill for making money. My daughter, my son, and I got a performing license so we could entertain people at Newport on the Levee, a gathering spot across the river in Kentucky. One day we went there to perform for tips. I had taught both my kids how to make some new balloon animals. My son, Javan, blew up the balloons. My daughter, Sierra, made animals and other figures while interacting with the children who came up. I did magic and made some pretty cool balloon creations myself to draw a crowd.

We had a blast, but fulfilling requests in the hot sun was hard work. After two hours, we had thirty-three dollars in tips piled in our performance bucket. Later, when we returned to the car, I asked my kids how we should divide the money. Their first reaction was to divide it equally: eleven dollars for each of us.

I said, "Wait. Before we do that, let me ask you a question. Did we all do equal work?" My son shuffled his feet. My daughter blurted out, "No we didn't! Javan blew up balloons for a while but then goofed off for at least half the time." Javan admitted that at least some of that was true. They were willing to admit that Dad did a lot more than either of them.

I suggested that Javan be given nine dollars, Sierra eleven dollars, and thirteen dollars should go to me. This payment plan was more in line with our efforts. Although everyone had worked, not everyone had worked as hard as the others. This pay would be less equal, but more fair.

At first, the kids were upset that we would not all be paid equally. But after a great discussion about fairness versus equality, everyone agreed to my proposal. Then I asked them to each pay me one dollar for parking, since it cost us three dollars to park. I also explained that out of the thirteen dollars

I had earned, I had to deduct nine dollars for the cost of the balloons. That left me with four dollars profit. Going out to practice our skills with balloons to entertain people afforded me a great opportunity to teach the kids about the hidden expenses facing a business owner.

In the end, I gave each of my kids half of my profits, leaving myself with nothing. In that way I was able to model generosity. It was my money (property rights), which I had earned (the gift of work). The profit (incentive) enabled me to freely give (generosity). It was my choice and my pleasure to give away my profits while reinforcing the biblical ideas behind capitalism.

My son now had incentive to work harder next time, since he saw the two-dollar difference between his work ethic and my daughter's more diligent effort. My daughter was rewarded for her additional focus. All of us enjoyed some time together and dreamed of ways to draw a bigger crowd the next time. The lesson was clear: pay people fairly, not equally.

A guideline for managers and employers

Employers need to treat their people fairly. In a business environment, greater producers deserve to receive greater rewards, as compared to those who produce less. When an employer pays everyone the same amount, it does away with incentive and also steals from those who produce more. The best producers are cheated out of a portion of their rightful profits.

The Bible tells us to pay our employees fairly for their honest work (see Proverbs 31:31). This is the beauty of capitalism's emphasis on individualism, incentive, and reward, which stands in stark contrast to the "group think" and "group reward" of socialism and communism.

Andrew Carnegie came to America from Scotland as a small boy. At first he did a variety of odd jobs, but eventually he became head of the largest steel manufacturer in the United States. At one time he was the wealthiest man in America and had forty-three millionaires working for him. (A million dollars in his day would be equivalent to at least twenty million dollars today.) When a newspaper reporter asked Carnegie how he had managed to hire forty-three millionaires, Carnegie smiled and responded, "They weren't millionaires when they started working for me."

The reporter's next question was, "What's your secret to developing leaders?" Carnegie said people are developed the same way gold is mined. Tons of dirt need to be moved to find an ounce of gold. But you don't go into a mine looking for dirt; you go looking for the gold. During the thankless work of moving piles of dirt, a leader must stay focused on the gold that is hidden there.[2]

Don't look for the flaws and blemishes in the people who work in your business. Work instead to develop the raw materials represented by your employees as you move a lot of dirt out of the way. See potential and possibility in your people. Serve your employees and your customers by developing the resource of your company's staff.

God does this. He looks beyond the surface of our flaws and brokenness. Instead, He sees us as highly valued vessels whom He alone can shape and mold. God found us in our dirt and grime. He found us while we were unkind, unloving, lacking self-control, and filled with fear and pride. He saw all the dirt. But in spite of the dust and filth, He entered into the caves of our lives in the person of Jesus Christ. He dwelt among us and offered us two things: His forgiveness and His leadership. He said to us, "Let me forgive all the dirt and grime in your life. I can forgive you. I can cover the blemishes. I can remove the stains. I can move the piles of dirt that were dumped on you, along with the filth you freely chose. I want to come in and lead your life, develop your potential, and give you the values of My wisdom, My grace, My strength, and My guidance. If you accept Me as Forgiver and Leader, I can lead you to discover real life, real prosperity, and real freedom."

Andrew Carnegie practiced similar values. How did his employees who became millionaires feel toward their boss—the man who polished them, trained them, and turned them into rich men? They loved him for giving them the opportunity to learn and succeed. They wanted to please him because of what he had done for them.

The same is true of God. Christ came to earth and was rejected in the dirty grime of the Cross in order to make fallen humanity heirs to the biggest fortune in the universe.

> For you did not receive the spirit of bondage again to fear, but you received the Spirit of adoption by whom we cry out, "Abba, Father."
> The Spirit Himself bears witness with our spirit that we are children of God, and if children, then heirs—heirs of God and joint heirs with Christ. (Romans 8:15–17)

You and I can be on the inheritance list of the richest Person in the galaxy. This life is filled with real meaning as we give to others in response to how Christ gave to us. We invest in others the way He invested in us. We stand for liberty, prosperity, and generosity.

God revealed the principles that form the foundation of a free society and a free-market economy: the gift of work, recognition of property rights, and incentives for greater productivity. These were expounded on by philosopher Adam Smith and guided the founders of our nation. But long before that, they were initiated by God.

PART 3

If God Were Talking to Economist John Maynard Keynes

What Would God Say to John Maynard Keynes About Spending?

How an economic system based on consumption violates biblical teaching

George Washington died the same way America's economy was brought to the brink of collapse during the recent Great Recession.

The first president of the United States was bled to death while under a doctor's care. As his symptoms grew worse, doctors siphoned out yet another pint of blood. At that time, physicians believed bad blood was a cause of serious health problems. With every pint pumped from his veins, Washington grew weaker, surprising the doctors. As their patient continued to decline, the educated medical professionals never questioned their bloodletting assumptions. Instead, they concluded they had not intervened enough. So they siphoned yet another pint of blood.

Washington's doctors killed him. His worsening symptoms were never interpreted as the proverbial light on the dashboard. Common sense was clamoring, "This is not working! Stop! You're not solving the problem!" Today politicians, elected officials, bureaucrats, and special-interest groups are bleeding the strength out of America. Just as flawed medical procedure killed President Washington, today an off-base economic theory is bankrupting our nation. The prevailing economic assumption that ushered in the lengthy Great Recession goes like this:

- America can never spend too little.
- The federal government can never intervene too soon.
- The government can never do too much to try to stimulate a sluggish economy.

The failed medical treatment administered to George Washington helps us to understand why the course of action that brought about the Great Recession is not the course of action that will put an end to it. But governments are slow to learn, and those who are committed to the economic theory of John Maynard Keynes are not likely to admit that the prescribed remedy is the thing that is killing us.

Keynes developed the economic theory that calls for far-reaching government interference in the free-market system. His failed prescription is "Keep spending! Keep borrowing! Keep inflating!" And like President Washington on his deathbed, I can almost hear America begging the federal government, "Please, stop helping. We can't take it!"

Almost everything Keynes taught about national economic policies is the opposite of what God has shown us. Yet Keynesian economic theory guided US presidents Herbert Hoover, Franklin Delano Roosevelt, George H. W. Bush, Bill Clinton, George W. Bush, and Barack Obama. America could have a growing, resilient economy if our nation's leaders had instead followed God's wisdom as echoed by thinkers such as Adam Smith. Instead, our country and its citizens, including you and me, are hurting needlessly due to wrongheaded ideas being played out year after year across our nation.

An apt analogy is to look at families that suffer due to bad judgment and financial mismanagement. I have seen the extreme pain of couples divorcing and splitting up their families because of excessive debt. I have seen tremendous pressure put on married couples due to chronic worry over their out-of-control spending. I have seen the nasty side of families at the funeral of a parent, when the heirs start bickering and seeking leverage to get a larger share of Mom's stuff. Men have sat in my office terrified that the secret credit cards their wives don't know about were about to come to light, knowing those cards would torpedo their marriage.

Despite the inevitable pain caused by ignoring God's wisdom on handling money, people look at the mess our nation's economy is in and ask, "What went wrong? How did we get into such a huge mess?" I'll give you the answer in just three words: John Maynard Keynes.

If you have studied economics, you are already familiar with the man whose economic theory has guided US presidents for generations. But maybe I can offer some perspectives that you have not considered before. Keynes taught a view of economics that focuses on spending, consuming, borrowing, and inflating. He promised that a government could offset the slowdown of an economic slump through increased spending (with the money borrowed from future Americans), by devaluing the dollar, and by taxing producers of goods and services at an incrementally higher rate.

He proposed these measures as actions for governments—temporary actions needed to bring a slow economy back to health. But we know from hard experience what happens when governments at all levels—cities, counties, states, and even boards of education and "special taxing districts"—ask voters to approve a temporary tax increase. Once the immediate crisis is addressed through higher taxes, other "needs" quickly surface, and the authorities justify extending the higher tax. This approach can be traced back to Keynes. He promised that government overspending and currency inflation would lead to economic prosperity, which would enable the federal government to discontinue increased spending and borrowing, and to restore the value of the dollar.

Consuming and Borrowing

The wisdom of the Scriptures shows us that financial health and stability is built on producing and profiting. But Keynes believed in building an economy on consuming and borrowing. He essentially said, "It's good policy to spend your way out of an economic crisis. When a country gets into trouble economically, turn on the printing presses and produce more currency."

The trouble with Keynes's theory is that it is based on borrowing and consuming rather than producing and saving. The Keynesian approach creates the illusion of a productive economy without producing very much of value. Here's an example to contrast the borrowing/consuming theory with that of producing/saving.

One day an American tourist stepped out of a taxi and walked into a hotel lobby in a small town in Europe. He pulled out a hundred-dollar bill to pay the hotel owner. He was given a key, and a bellhop escorted him upstairs so he could inspect his room. The hotel owner, meanwhile, took the hundred-dollar bill and ran to pay his debt with the butcher. The butcher headed out the back door with the money and ran to pay his debt to a pig farmer. The pig farmer hurried into town to pay his debt to the supplier of his animal feed. The supplier used the hundred-dollar bill to pay the hotel owner for the room he had rented a week earlier to celebrate his wedding anniversary.

Just as the hotel owner was putting the original hundred-dollar bill into the hotel safe, the tourist came downstairs after inspecting the room. He was not satisfied with the accommodations, and he demanded a full cash refund. Although nothing was produced in this economic exchange, the town's leading citizens were out of debt.

Money was exchanged in a circular fashion to pay, after the fact, for goods and services that had been previously purchased on credit. Business owners had built the local economy on credit rather than on producing and profit. And the hotel owner, who offered lodging and had received payment in advance from the tourist, ended up with nothing when the tourist changed his mind about spending the night. The bill owed by the feed-store owner was marked "paid," but the hotel safe never got to hold the hundred-dollar bill.

This is a simple, comical example of how Keynes's economic philosophy generates an empty illusion rather than the hard reality of sustainable growth and prosperity. Our nation and its people are suffering as a result, which is why Godonomics is needed now more than ever to reverse the decline.

A Businesswoman Leads the Way

Earlier we discussed the businesswoman portrayed in the thirty-first chapter of Proverbs. The woman is entrepreneurial, hard working, generous, savvy, and great at relationships, among other things. She offers a useful case study in the everyday application of the core principles of Godonomics:

- The woman began with producing, not a Keynesian approach of spending and borrowing. She found a vineyard capable of producing grapes and assessed its suitability as a part of her bigger business plan (see Proverbs 31:16).
- The woman profited from her work, which is characterized in the Bible as a good thing (see verse 16). Although the story being told took place in ancient times, the woman had the advantage of personal liberty, which is central to a free-market system. She was careful to meet customer needs as "she perceives that her merchandise is good" (verse 18).
- From her previous profits she produced savings (see verse 16), and her savings enabled her to invest in another vineyard. The business expansion produced jobs for more workers. It also increased her business's capacity to produce more (see verse 16).
- In addition to investing profits back into the business, the businesswoman used a portion of her savings to share with those in need (see verse 20).

The businesswoman did not have to comply with the dictates of a centralized authority. She enjoyed the freedom to make her own decisions about her business, including the product line, business expansion, and how she used the profits—in investing, giving, or spending.

Godonomics offers a stark contrast to the consumer-onomics of John

Maynard Keynes. The last American president who held to the principles of limited government and free enterprise was Calvin Coolidge. It was during his administration that the Roaring Twenties were ushered in; Coolidge kept his word and prevented the federal government from meddling with the nation's economy. He inherited a financial mess and turned it around using a common-sense approach that is consistent with Godonomics. In the book *Silent Cal's Almanack,* David Pietrusza lays out the case.

> Because every politician who wants to obtain office says "I'm going to do four or five things: I'm going to cut taxes, I'm going to reduce waste in government, I'm going to cut the debt, and I'm going to bring you prosperity and everybody is going to have a job and there's going to be no inflation."... We fall for it every stinking time and they never do it.

During the crisis of Coolidge's time, Calvin resisted the temptation to follow the Keynesian recipe of government spending and intervention. Instead of using the federal government as the rescuer responsible to stimulate the economy, he practiced the free-enterprise concepts that David Pietrusza noted. In contrast to the empty promises of previous politicians, Silent Cal resisted the pressure to spend. Instead, he reduced waste, cut taxes, and reduced debt.

> And Calvin Coolidge did all of those things. And then, the historians and the pundits say, he was in office for six years and didn't do a d--n thing. No, he refrained from that. He refrained from pouring federal money into [the economy].[1]

The presidents following Coolidge put their confidence in government regulations and centralized control, in addition to Keynesian policies such as an emphasis on consuming rather than producing. When you consume more than you produce, you incur debt. Since you haven't built up savings, you turn to borrowing. When an individual borrows money, the result is usually enslavement to compounded interest, which binds the person to years of debt. In the case of the federal government, however, three options are available:

Option 1: Finance increased government consumption (spending) through taxing the citizens, who are the producers. This generates revenue for the government as it decreases the profits of citizens who are producing goods and services. By reducing profits through taxation, the government decreases personal savings as well as the cash reserves of businesses. This inhibits the ability of businesses to expand and hire more employees.

Option 2: The federal government inflates the currency. This is done by devaluing the dollar, which hurts the poor and anyone living on a fixed income. It also hurts Americans in general who see the buying power of their wages decline. Inflating the currency is a direct violation of God's prohibitions against "dishonest scales" and His requirements for "just weight[s]" (Proverbs 11:1; compare Leviticus 19:36).

Option 3: Borrow money from other nations, ignoring God's commands against doing just that (see Deuteronomy 28:15–45, [especially verses 33, 43–44]). The debtor nation cannot avoid sacrificing its autonomy and giving the creditor nation power over its affairs.

None of these three options is in line with God's commands. Each one passes the buck of today's irresponsible spending to our children and grandchildren.

My grandfather, Robert Hovind, started early in teaching my father the lesson of not buying something until you could afford it. When my father was young and wanted to buy a toy, my grandpa would buy it and immediately place it, still unopened, on a shelf in the living room. My dad could not have use of the toy until he had paid for it, so he worked small jobs and did chores to earn money to pay for the toy. When the day came that my dad had earned the purchase, he enjoyed and valued it so much more.

My father passed on these lessons to me and my siblings. I started working as a soccer referee when I was twelve. I made four dollars per game, perched on a stepladder making calls on infractions of the rules of indoor soccer. That was four dollars per hour. When the family went out for pizza and my dad would pay the twenty-dollar charge for the meal, he would announce, "This pizza cost *five hours* on the soccer referee's ladder." We teased him about his repeated speech. But years later I realized he was teaching us the value of money—the connection between earning and spending. He was teaching us to not consume at a level that exceeds the money we earn.

Consuming at a level that exceeds what you produce feeds an insatiable appetite, both for individuals and for our nation. Since governments have no

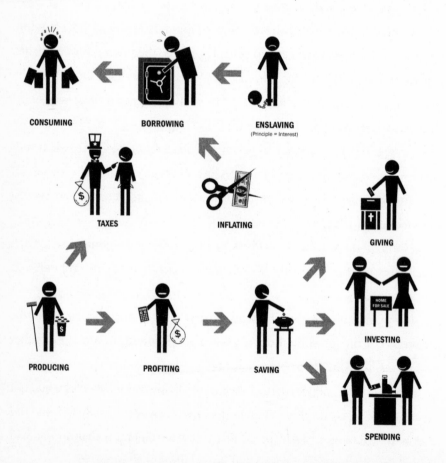

money, they always consume. Notice the flow chart of money in the illustration. Governments borrow money by taking from producers through taxation, receiving money from inflation, or getting money from other nations by enslaving themselves to credit.

Notice the arrows in the flow chart moving from enslaving to borrowing. When the federal government spends more money than exists in the US Treasury, it has to borrow money through the sale of government obligations. Many of those obligations are owned by citizens, but they are also purchased by other nations, committing future generations of Americans to pay for today's overconsumption. Today's irresponsible decisions enslave future Americans to the task of repaying unimaginable debt owed to foreign nations.

Individuals and families do this as well. We consume more than we produce. We end up borrowing by taking money from the future and enslaving ourselves to future debt payments.

In Godonomics, however, the available options do not include overconsuming and then burdening others with the resulting debt. Instead, the focus is always on others' needs. To make a profit from the production of goods and services, we focus on consumers' needs. Profits make it possible to accumulate savings, which are spent in part on goods and services produced by others. Savings are also invested in business expansion, new jobs, helping the needy, and doing the work of God around the world. The emphasis from start to finish is on others.

The emphasis of Keynesian consumer-onomics is the exact opposite. It benefits those who are in power while destroying freedom and prosperity for everyone else. The federal government—with the power to tax, borrow, and devalue the dollar—is the beneficiary of consumer-driven economics. Governments do not produce; they consume. Governments have no money; they can only redirect the money that is taken from others.

As of this writing, the United States is more than sixteen and one-half

US NATIONAL DEBT		DEBT PER CITIZEN	DEBT PER TAXPAYER
$16,509,499,026,892		$ 52,363	$ 146,101
US FEDERAL SPENDING		US FEDERAL BUDGET DEFICIT	
$ 3,539,577,864,657		$ 1,063,333,369,108	

From US Debt Clock.org. Current as of February 2013.

trillion dollars in debt. That is a measure from a fixed point in time. It does not include as much as ten times that amount that is owed in future payouts of promised benefits, such as Social Security and Medicare payments, veterans' benefits, and Medicaid.[2]

Remember our working definitions of capitalism and socialism?

- *Capitalism:* the free exchange of privately owned goods and services
- *Socialism:* state control and state ownership of industry and property

Consumer-onomics gives control to a centralized authority, the federal government. Since the government is granted power to tax, borrow, and inflate, it uses those powers to benefit the elite at the expense of the citizens. This is in line with the ideology of socialism. Those who wield power funnel money from the citizens to the centralized authority, the government. And those who hold positions of power in the government stand to receive direct benefits. This can take many forms, from pushing regulations or legislation that favor an industry that is a donor to an officeholder's campaign to using government connections to line up lucrative opportunities following a term of government service.

Keynes's system banks on tax policies that confiscate a significant portion of your wealth to be used by people you did not elect for purposes you oppose. This is in direct opposition to the teachings of Adam Smith and the wisdom found in the Bible. In contrast, Godonomics offers you, your family, your company, and our nation as a whole the chance to experience liberty and prosperity and to practice generosity according to the dictates of a person's own convictions.

We Overspend Our Way to Slavery, Not Prosperity

Keynesian economics leads to the slavery of society's producers—you, me, and everyone else who works, earns, profits, saves, invests, and produces goods or services in the US economy. I don't mean *slavery* in the sense of one individual owning another individual, but slavery in the sense of losing one's freedom in the financial arena. Proverbs 22:7 exposes a reality that Keynes's consumer-onomics will never tell you. Lenders exercise amazing power over those who are foolish enough to borrow. Our grandparents knew this, and they tried to instill in us habits of living that would enable us to escape financial slavery. They told us things like "Don't spend more than you make" and "Save some money for a rainy day."

If you ignore the wisdom contained in such advice, you will invite pressure of a type that will overshadow the things you love most: your health, your peace of mind, and your harmonious relationships with your spouse and children. It can all be traced back to one choice and the actions that resulted from that choice: you spent too much. You took on too large a mortgage to buy a house. You took out a couple of auto loans so you and your spouse could drive better cars. You took out a home-equity loan to do some remodeling and bought furniture and carpeting and appliances and electronics on credit. You made purchases that you couldn't afford, and now the payments on your debt control your life by limiting your choices and limiting your generosity. Every month those payments eat away at your take-home pay. You overspent your way to slavery, not prosperity!

The Bible warns that we overspend our way to slavery, not prosperity. But Keynes tried to flip this around. His economic theory seeks to solve the problem of a nation's debt with the remedy of spending and borrowing even more. He believed you could spend your way to prosperity.

Here is another astounding quote from his bizarre approach to sound fiscal policy: "If you owe your bank manager a thousand pounds, you are at his mercy. If you owe him a million pounds, he is at your mercy."[3]

You see what Keynes is saying? If you have spent more than you can afford and the bank is breathing down your neck, you need to spend and borrow even more. If you can borrow millions instead of thousands, the lender will be at your mercy.

But this is utter nonsense! You are broke and worse than broke! You are enslaved to debt. Going deeper into debt can never make you more secure financially. It does only one thing: it makes you more broke, more enslaved. What assets you possess are worthless since they are more than offset by your debt.

My wife, Beth, used to worry about money. While growing up she saw the tension in her parents' marriage caused by money issues. But recently I found out that her mom and dad were able to eventually get on top of their financial struggles. When they paid off the last of their credit-card debt, Beth's parents gathered their credit cards and had a card-cutting party. It was a way to celebrate their financial freedom.

God's wisdom exposes the lie of Keynesian economics: "Owe no one anything except to love one another, for he who loves another has fulfilled the law" (Romans 13:8).

Though our culture has bought into the belief that there are no absolute truths, reality teaches us otherwise. Everyday experience shows us that we don't neutralize God's laws when we argue against them, ignore them, or choose to live in opposition to them. God makes it clear: "Just as the rich rule the poor, *so the borrower is servant to the lender*" (Proverbs 22:7, NLT). That is Scripture's way of stating an unvarying economic principle: "You overspend your way to slavery, not prosperity." You can borrow and live it up...for a while, but eventually reality catches up with you. There are people who are still paying credit-card interest on "must-have" items they have since sold in garage sales. This principle is true for nations as well as individuals. Here is how God says it:

> The LORD will open to you His good treasure, the heavens, to give the rain to your land in its season, and to bless all the work of your hand. You shall lend to many nations, *but you shall not borrow.* (Deuteronomy 28:12)

Then God spells out the unavoidable consequences that follow when a nation refuses to adhere to His instructions:

> The alien who is among you shall rise higher and higher above you, and you shall come down lower and lower. He shall lend to you, but you shall not lend to him; he shall be the head, and you shall be the tail.
>
> Moreover all these curses shall come upon you and pursue and overtake you, until you are destroyed, because you did not obey the voice of the LORD your God, to keep His commandments and His statutes which He commanded you. (Deuteronomy 28:43–45)

God challenged ancient Israel to trust Him to meet the nation's needs rather than relying on the treasure houses of other nations. He warned that borrowing from other nations would lead to a loss of national sovereignty.

In 1956, Britain was a debtor nation that had to cede power to the United States. That year, Britain and France were battling Egypt over control of the Suez Canal. The Soviet Union was threatening to intervene on behalf of Egypt. The United States wanted to avoid military action, so it demanded that Britain and France withdraw from the region. That request was denied.

The United States then increased the pressure by waging financial war-fare. America had loaned so much money to England that the US by 1956 owned much of England's debt. In response to the tensions over the Suez Canal, America (the lender) told England (the borrower) to give up control of the canal, threatening to sell off US holdings of the British pound if Eng-land refused to comply. Such an action could have destroyed England's econ-omy. Soon after, England pulled out of Egypt because it was enslaved to the United States.

But today the situation is reversed, with America giving up its national sovereignty by borrowing heavily from other nations, most notably China. At the level of personal finances, some have called this the two-cent rule. The difference between a rich person and a poor person is two cents. If two people each make one dollar, and one of them makes a habit of spending ninety-nine cents out of every dollar while the other spends one dollar and one cent, the overspender slowly becomes more and more enslaved. The saver who spends less than the amount earned slowly becomes freer and richer. One enjoys in-creasing prosperity, while the other slides into economic slavery through in-creasing indebtedness.

No matter how much money you earn, you must learn to entrust your future to God and His wisdom. God wants you to experience liberty, free-dom, and joy. He doesn't want you to suffer the bondage of debt. The way to enjoy the former and avoid the latter is to live within your means by "acting your wage."

What Would God Say to John Maynard Keynes About Budgeting?

There is only one proven way to live within your means

How do we overcome the appetite that tells us we deserve to have more than our income will allow? How can we resist the tendency to borrow rather than save? Godonomics offers three steps to "acting your own wage": Look Inward, Look Backward, and Look Forward.

Step One: Look Inward

The first step is to look deep inside and ask, "Why?" Why do we spend more than we make? If we are honest with ourselves and we take the Bible seriously, answering this question will reveal an idol. There is something we value more than God, and that something is what reigns in our hearts. The most common idols in the American culture are SPAM (Status, Performance, Appearance, and Money.) As a lover of Monty Python, I see Spamalot all over the Camelot of America.

For instance, if I define my value by others' approval, I will be more likely to overspend in an attempt to earn the admiration of others. If I believe that status is the end game of my heart, my brain will hijack common sense by chanting, "Think what others will think when they see me in that house, driving that car, and wearing those clothes."

Until we answer the "why" question regarding our unwise spending, common-sense financial planning will always be trumped by our heart's illegitimate role as puppet master. The Bible says that until we place God at the center of our lives and acknowledge that He is the Source of our approval and identity, we will constantly be tempted to chase "things" that we wrongly believe will give our lives meaning. Jesus said it this way: "Where your treasure is, there your heart will be also" (Luke 12:34).

Every culture offers enough false treasures to keep people spending money they don't have in a vain attempt to replace God with an idol. Some cultures elevate honor and others beauty. Some turn sexual intimacy into the highest goal. When you take inventory of your heart, keep in mind that the cultural values that most easily lure us are *good* things. But we can pursue them with such single-minded devotion that we turn them into *ultimate* things. As long as our hearts are in love with control, status, appearance, performance, image, or wealth, our habits will follow those misguided longings—even if we realize the resulting decisions are unwise.

There's a wabbit behind our habits. Remember Elmer Fudd going wabbit hunting in the old Bugs Bunny cartoons? He knew there was a wabbit under the ground, and he went looking for it. We must do the same; there is always a wabbit under the surface of our habits that must be exposed to find spiritual and financial freedom.

We can try to work harder to stay within a budget. We can educate ourselves about wise financial management. However, promising ourselves that we will do better is never the solution. We must first deal with the matter of what our hearts seek after. When money or clothes or respect is our god, we will consume and borrow in order to feed our god. But our gods will never be satisfied.

Looking inward gives us a chance to find the god that drives us. To identify this god we have to take a hard and thorough personal inventory. In fact, all the other steps will have little effect if we don't look inward first. This is true both individually and nationally. We need fiscal responsibility. We need to reject Keynesian nonsense and live within our means. Then we can move to Step Two, where we look backward.

Step Two: Look Backward

When we look backward, we can see that overspending and borrowing to finance our desire to consume didn't make us happier, freer, or more generous. Overspending did just the opposite: it created more pressure and allowed us less freedom. Debt compounds our problems. We work longer hours to try to compensate, which steals our time and leads to more health problems. Secrets multiply as we try to hide the extent of our overspending.

It's necessary to look backward so we can examine and learn from the destructive patterns of the past. I bought a copy of Quicken, a computer program that tracks my spending. It makes it easy to look backward. It's painful but truthful. Quicken tells me that I go to a lot of movies. It reveals that I eat out an awful lot.

If you get to the end of a paycheck and wonder, *Where did it all go?*, now is the time to get a system to look backward. Money patterns won't change without you making them change.

Twelve-step groups call it the insane cycle: doing the same thing over and over while expecting a different outcome. The Bible describes it in a more earthy way: "As a dog returns to his own vomit, so a fool repeats his folly" (Proverbs 26:11). This pattern applies to an alcoholic promising himself he won't take another drink and then finding himself lying in his own vomit. It applies as well to repeating destructive economic practices. The big difference between the two is that an entire nation of citizens can be ruined financially by the policies of Keynesian political leaders.

The economy went out drinking in the late 1990s, investing heavily in dotcom ventures, only a few of which paid off. But that wasn't all. Low interest rates encouraged overspending, and America decided that borrowing from other nations tasted great. As the market attempted to recalibrate in 2000, George W. Bush and Federal Reserve chairman Alan Greenspan decided to help sober up both Main Street and Wall Street—by passing out more liquor! Remember the stimulus checks that came in the mail? They didn't stimulate much of anything. Nor did low-interest adjustable-rate mortgages benefit mortgage holders who couldn't afford the dramatic increases in their payments five years later. Vice President Dick Cheney said we shouldn't worry about deficits, and our country hit the wall.

Through the pain of a major reality check in 2008, we had the potential to sober up. Stocks sank, the market shook, and cracks appeared in the wall. Fed chief Ben Bernanke had taken over for Greenspan, and President Barack Obama had taken over for President Bush. But the new leaders chose to operate out of the same playbook. They inflated the currency by printing more money. They continued to borrow from China. They submitted spending plans to Congress that ran so deeply in the red that we are passing on unimaginable payment requirements to our grandchildren.

And that wasn't the end of it. They pushed for legislation to bail out companies that, according to the rules of free-market capitalism, needed to go out of business, or at least to restructure and downsize through managed bankruptcy. This was short-term, apply-a-bandage thinking. It was repeating the mistakes of the past, applying the same failed solutions that had gotten us into this mess. It is what Proverbs calls foolishness, applied to the nation's economic policy.

God says, "The prudent sees the evil and hides himself, but the naive go on, and are punished for it" (Proverbs 22:3, NASB). Well, here we are. The rate of unemployment remained at dangerously high levels in spite of federal efforts to bring it down.

President Obama's campaign team in 2012 painted his jobs record in the best possible light. One campaign ad stated that employers had "added 3.1

million jobs since Obama took office, a claim fact-checked and verified by ABC News." But even with that, there still had been "a net loss of more than a million jobs since Obama began his [first] term."[1]

Keynesian politicians from both sides of the aisle promise, again, that they can stimulate the economy with the passage of another so-called jobs bill. But drinking more liquor is never the way to sober up. We need to take the painful steps required for a national twelve-step program. Delaying the pain only inflates the pain bubble that will burst later.

A few years ago, *Saturday Night Live* did a sketch with Steve Martin that showed the wisdom of God's blueprint and the idiocy of John Keynes'. It's an advertisement for a book titled *Don't Buy Stuff You Cannot Afford*. The couple in the sketch struggles to understand the concept, even though the spokesman for the book keeps repeating it: "Don't buy stuff you cannot afford."[2]

Wouldn't that simple advice save us a boatload of trouble?

So is debt always bad? Should we consider taking on debt for certain purposes? Is paying interest always morally wrong? Isn't lending money at interest forbidden by the Bible? Let's look backward.

In about 400 BC, Aristotle taught that money was sterile and nonproductive. He, like other Greek gnostics, believed the material world was inherently evil. He taught that pursuing money and productivity was creating a yoke that bound a person to a wicked world. This worldview infiltrated the early church while Paul and Peter continually tried to differentiate Gnosticism from biblical Christianity. However, the influence of Gnosticism was hard to eradicate. Leaders in the Roman Catholic Church taught that charging interest at any level was usury (the practice of lending money at unreasonably high rates) and was therefore forbidden. Though some biblical passages, such as Exodus 22:25 and Deuteronomy 23:19–20, suggest that charging any interest at all is usury, many other passages, such as Matthew 25 and Luke 19, instruct otherwise.

Church reformer John Calvin questioned the idea that all interest was usury, just as he challenged the Gnostic worldview that condemned material wealth. Calvin submitted that if God created the world to be a productive place, then it could be used for God's glory. If God came and lived among us, which He did in Jesus Christ, it was further evidence that the material world was not inherently evil (as the Gnostics claimed) or an illusion (as Eastern religions suggested).

Calvin reasoned that though the creation was broken by the ripple impact of original sin, it was not entirely evil. Calvin noted that God came into creation in human flesh, which was ultimate proof that matter was not bad. He showed the church that people's real needs (physical, emotional, mental, and spiritual) are realities that the followers of Christ must take seriously.

Calvin also disputed Aristotle's idea that money was unproductive and evil. Knowing that money could be exceedingly productive, he called into question the Roman Catholic teachings that defined all interest as usury. While a case can be made that the church had condemned the charging of interest to help protect people from exploitation, Calvin saw that classifying all interest charges as usury was neither right nor biblical. He noted that Jesus, in two of His parables, spoke of putting money in the bank to gain interest (see Mathew 25:14–30, especially verse 27; Luke 19:12–27, especially verse 23). Calvin redefined usury as the charging of *excessive* interest, emphasizing the Golden Rule as the standard for conducting economic transactions.[3]

The church reformer, by freeing money and capital from the prison of a misguided worldview, unleashed the fuel necessary for production. Now, with the potential of interest as a reward for investment, there was great incentive to risk capital on new ventures. A wave of investment began to sweep the world. By looking backward, Calvin changed economic history.

In learning to act our own wage, we have to first look inward to repair the heart problem, and then look backward to identify repetitive destructive behaviors and wrong economic thinking. Now let's examine the third step by looking forward.

Step Three: Look Forward

As we look forward to identify what is essential, few things are as important as *margin*. However, it is almost extinct in the lives of American families. Margin is the renewable resource that helps protect our families, our marriages, and our mental health. The principle behind it is simple: you are careful in advance to avoid filling all your time, finances, and emotional energies to capacity. Instead, you are intentional about leaving space available, or margin, in those critical areas. That way, when you encounter the inevitable unexpected circumstances of life, you aren't pushed beyond your limits.[4]

Instead of prioritizing margin, we live on the edge. We crowd our schedules with so much activity that we have little time left for family, friendship, and rest. And with our finances, we spend all we have and then some. We don't keep back reserves for the unexpected. The wisdom of Godonomics advises us to make sure we set aside margin in our budgets and our lives as we look to the future.

God recommends careful advance planning:

The plans of the diligent lead surely to advantage, but everyone who is hasty comes surely to poverty. (Proverbs 21:5, NASB)

Four things are small on the earth, but they are exceedingly wise:
The ants are not a strong people, but they prepare their food in the summer. (Proverbs 30:24–25, NASB)

It is not easy to commit to creating margin in our lives. We must prepare to push back from a culture obsessed with overconsumption. It's important to realize that one result of not acting our wage is that we spend all our financial resources, leaving nothing to share with those who need help.

You must be prepared for the criticism that will come if you choose to put margin in your life. If you decide you can no longer afford the mortgage you're paying and you move to a more modest house, others will say, "If you downsize, people will think your business is in trouble." If you decide to get out from under a costly auto loan, you will hear, "Think of all the embarrassing conversations you'll need to have if you sell your new car and drive an older model."

One businessman whom I counseled knew he had a hard decision at hand. Although his business was going well, reducing financial and time demands in his personal life seemed to be the wise, healthy path to take. He asked himself, "Do I choose margin or status? Do I endure the pressure of living at the limit or swim into the calming waters of deeper contentment?"

Over the next few months, he and his wife decided to buy a house that was half the size of their former home. Within a few months, the husband was working fewer hours, and the family was facing less stress and experiencing a lot more joy in life. Plus, they were excited about their new freedom to be more generous with their money.

The question of debt

As we look forward, being intentional about wise planning, these questions must be raised: Is *all* debt contrary to God's teachings? Are there allowable exceptions, such as a home mortgage or business loan?

Howard Dayton, a Christian financial educator, advises us to use debt conservatively, providing three important guidelines:

1. The item purchased is an asset with potential to appreciate in value or to produce an income.

2. The value of the item equals or exceeds the amount owed against it.

3. The debt is not so large that repayment puts undue strain on the budget.[5]

Here is another way to think about debt. A business loan is an investment in an entrepreneurial activity that shows promise over time of producing income. A car loan, on the other hand, enables the "purchase" of an item that loses value the minute you're handed the key. One has the potential of producing income that will far exceed the cost of interest paid on the loan. The other will not retain a value that exceeds the cost of taking out the loan.

If we want to experience freedom from debt and anxiety over money, it will require taking a countercultural approach. God's wisdom leads to the true prosperity of having real savings, money-producing assets, and the freedom of margin. God's wisdom liberates us to stop chasing the next thing and actually enjoy what we already have. We get to own things without their owning us. We can't allow ourselves to be driven to work harder and acquire more things because of discontentment!

Remember, we overspend our way to slavery, not prosperity. And the way to get off the destructive path of overspending is to act your own wage!

PART 4

If God Were Talking to President Franklin Delano Roosevelt

What Would God Say to FDR About Unintended Consequences?

We have to face the future outcomes of faulty assumptions

Several years ago I saw a movie that gave me nightmares. Produced by former US comptroller general David Walker and a bipartisan group, the movie *I.O.U.S.A.* attempts to explain America's seemingly unexplainable national debt. I watched the thirty-minute version rather than the full two-hour edition. In just half an hour there was more than enough terrifying news.[1]

Here is just one looming disaster that's likely to keep you awake at night: the cost of Social Security, Medicaid, and Medicare benefits is growing at such an incredible rate that in the near future, these three programs will consume the entire federal budget.

Appointed by President Bill Clinton and continuing to serve under George W. Bush, Walker sounded the alarm to warn of the tidal wave of debt. Having served under a Democratic and a Republican chief executive, he came to one conclusion: neither of the major political parties will stop excessive federal spending.

Walker shows in the documentary that the federal government keeps several sets of financial books. This means that when we hear about how bad the situation is, we haven't heard the half of it. The public is lied to by the Washington elite while taxpayers' hard-earned money is channeled into wasteful earmarks and unsustainable programs.

As I looked into this, I found that the word *politics* comes from two roots: *poly,* meaning "many," and *ticks,* meaning "blood-sucking parasites." Okay, maybe not, but it sure seems that way. Politicians have become a swarm of out-of-control spenders, leeching off today's taxpayers and piling up debt for future generations.

Whether you are a Democrat or a Republican, the facts are clear: we're in trouble. Taking small steps will not protect us from the avalanche of debt that continues growing as it gets closer to overtaking us. Rescuing our nation from economic collapse will require radical changes, significant modifications, and an iron will. We continue to spend far more than we can pay back. And this hard reality brings us to examine the legacy of President Franklin Delano Roosevelt.

What would God say to FDR, and why are we even asking? Roosevelt was president through the depths of the Great Depression, and he led the way in launching the New Deal, an ambitious and costly series of federal programs designed to address the suffering of a large segment of the American population. His efforts have been credited with bringing the nation out of its worst economic crisis, but is that view based on historical fact? And what of his legacy? Are we, today, paying the exorbitant price of decades of misguided federal largesse initiated by Roosevelt? Did the New Deal set in motion the very thing that is now threatening to suffocate America's future?

Roosevelt is a hero to many. He served as chief executive during two of the greatest threats to the United States: the Great Depression and World War II. He provided strong leadership and was a reassuring figure to many at a time when the world seemed to be coming apart. But whether you grew up loving FDR or holding him and his policies suspect, we can no longer ignore the realities we face today.

Throughout most of the twentieth century, the Keynesian model of overspending guided the thinking and policies of top leaders of both the Democratic and Republican parties. God's message to each of them would be simple but not easy to adopt: "Stop spending tomorrow's money today."

A firm policy of ensuring that federal spending does not exceed revenues would be much easier to enact and enforce if the opposite approach weren't so appealing—and so deceptive. The nearly irresistible attraction of borrowing rather than budgeting is the perception that borrowing works. It offers fulfillment of a fantasy: that government can do everything the people want and need, and do it right now. However, the truth is hidden in the shadows. Borrowing offers only a short-term substitute for a solution while delaying the painful consequences until later. We know this to be true because we can see the consequences before us today.

Our nation's recent history shows that one party wants to cut taxes but spends too much. The other party wants to raise taxes but spends too much. Godonomics challenges both Democrats and Republicans because, although they disagree on how to do it, lawmakers on both sides of the aisle are presuming upon tomorrow's revenues. Proverbs has some timely advice regarding their lack of discipline: "There is desirable treasure, and oil in the dwelling of the wise, but a foolish man squanders it" (Proverbs 21:20).

The wise man has oil in his dwelling. He has surplus. He has saved some of his profit.

The wise man limited the amount he used in order to have oil left over, held in reserve. This is called savings. But the foolish fail to plan ahead. They don't determine today's spending based on a realistic budget that leaves

PRODUCING   PROFITING   SAVING   INVESTING

resources available for future needs. Even worse, through the use of credit, the foolish spend tomorrow's money as well as what is available today. This applies at the level of individuals, families, cities, counties, states, and nations. The federal government exchanges borrowing for budgeting, passing the burden of repaying debt to our children and grandchildren.

The foolish are happy to pass the bill on to the next generation, a policy that stands in stark contrast to the wisdom of Godonomics. "A good man leaves an inheritance to his children's children" (Proverbs 13:22). The prudent work hard to produce and profit, leaving an inheritance to the next two generations. As we have seen in earlier chapters, the Bible does not condemn money and profit making. The more you make, the more you can bless future generations and, today, help the poor.

Contrast that with the foolish economic policies that guide the federal government. Not only do we not leave savings to our children and grandchildren, we borrow and obligate our grandchildren to the debts of their grandparents. It is foolish to spend all of today's money today. It is even more foolish to spend all of tomorrow's money today. It is *immoral* to spend someone else's money today. Our children and grandchildren will have less take home pay in the future, due to their having to pay the interest on our borrowing today.

The phrase *deficit spending* means spending tomorrow's money today. It means going into a hole and hoping someone will pay for it in the future. We find ourselves, more than seventy years after the end of the Great Depression, on the receiving end of much of the overspending that occurred during the New Deal.

Before we can assess what God would say to FDR, we must take a clear-eyed look at the facts surrounding the New Deal. Most history books portray Roosevelt's policies during the Great Depression along these lines: The United States was struggling to recover economically from the stock market crash of 1929. The economy continued to weaken, and the suffering of the people continued to spread. FDR took decisive action by developing an unprecedented number of federal programs that addressed joblessness, the struggles of old age, and the nation's infrastructure. These initiatives saved the day; however, they required that the federal government spend money it didn't have.

In addition to spending vast amounts on the Works Progress Administration, the Civilian Conservation Corps, the Tennessee Valley Authority, and other economic development and public-employment programs, Roosevelt launched the Social Security Administration to assist the elderly. Our history teachers told us this gamble—paying for programs developed in the 1930s using money borrowed from future taxpayers—got the United States out of the Great Depression.

We were also told that Herbert Hoover, who preceded FDR in the White House, was a free-market capitalist who ran the country into the ground. (Hoover was president when the stock market crashed in 1929.) FDR was credited with protecting the country from the evils of unfettered capitalism through the protective measures of massive government programs and activist political intervention and regulation.

Now let's examine the facts.

Hoover was not a free-market capitalist. In fact, during his four years in office, he increased deficit spending by 47 percent. The pressure of that overspending caused the Dow Jones Average to slide. As stocks were falling, Hoover continued his policy of overspending. Overspending created the artificial "boom" that went bust when the stock market collapsed.

Government spending almost always has a short-term benefit, followed by an unintended, longer-term bust. Further, government intervention always favors one group over others. So one group stands to benefit while all others suffer. A variety of factors contributed to the Great Depression. However, Hoover and Roosevelt share much of the blame through their meddling with the economy and the creation of costly, ill-advised federal programs.

Chris Edwards, director of tax policy for the Cato Institute, summarizes the problems:

> Misguided federal policies caused the downturn that began in 1929, and they prevented the economy from fully recovering for a decade. Policy blunders by the Federal Reserve, Congress, and Presidents Herbert Hoover and Roosevelt battered the economy on many fronts....
>
> Many people think that we need a big government to prevent, or to reverse, recessions. But the 1930s illustrate that activist policies increase, not decrease, economic instability.[2]

I counseled a married couple who had been high-school sweethearts. Just months after their wedding, a horrible secret came out. The husband had a heroin problem that he had kept hidden since the age of fourteen. The stress of being married pushed his addiction into overdrive. He sold equipment from his business to buy more heroin. This kept up until he had sold every piece of landscaping equipment, and then he turned to stealing from family members.

His wife sat in my living room, weeping, with her head buried in her hands. I led an intervention later in my office. The man's sister, his wife, and I confronted him. "You have to stop doing what you've been doing if you want to change."

Over the next two years I watched him change his patterns as he rebuilt his life. He surrendered his foolishness to God and asked God for His wisdom. He wanted to build his life on God's wisdom for life, for marriage, and for financial management. Now, ten years later, his marriage is stronger than ever, and he has found a full recovery. He suffered the consequences of his actions and was finally ready to make real, lasting change. It takes a strong will to make hard choices and to follow through with the necessary changes. Magically hoping things will be different doesn't change anything.

President Hoover followed the insane logic of doing the same thing over and over again while expecting a different result. As the pressure of his over-spending increased each year, he simply continued his policy of deficit spending. He did not demonstrate the restraint of a free-market capitalist. Hoover's financial bloodletting was killing the economy.

Edwards continues his analysis:

> In the early 1920s, Treasury Secretary Andrew Mellon ushered in an economic boom by championing income tax cuts that reduced the top individual rate from 73 to 25 percent. But the lessons of these successful tax cuts were forgotten as the economy headed downwards after 1929. President Hoover signed into law the Revenue Act of 1932, which was the largest peacetime tax increase in U.S. history. The act increased the top individual tax rate from 25 to 63 percent. After his election in 1932, Roosevelt imposed further individual and corporate tax increases. The highest individual rate was increased to 79 percent. State and local governments also increased taxes during the 1930s....
> All these tax increases killed incentives for work, investment, and entrepreneurship at a time when they were sorely needed.[3]

Roosevelt was elected to his first term as president in 1932, and he continued the failed policies of his predecessor. He launched the First New Deal, which required borrowing and spending incredible amounts of money to finance unprecedented government programs. His massive investment in public-works projects and other public-employment efforts produced a modest climb in the Dow Jones Average. Unfortunately, the temporary boost didn't elevate the Dow Jones to a level that came close to its previous high.

Still, Roosevelt decided that the temporary boost was reason enough for more of the same. So he pushed through a Second New Deal. The problem with getting drunk on deficit spending is tomorrow's hangover.

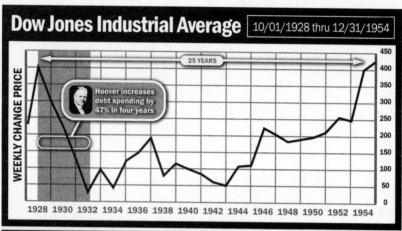

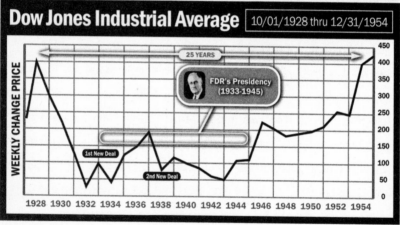

Ultimately, what goes up must come down. Roosevelt's second shot of adrenaline—in the form of even more deficit spending—was the proverbial straw that broke the camel's back, and the Second New Deal finally broke the system. How did this come about? Edwards offers further analysis:

> Many New Deal policies raised employer costs, contributing to the extraordinarily high unemployment of the 1930s. NIRA [National Industrial Recovery Act] industry codes required high wages. The new Social Security tax increased compensation costs. New minimum wage rules reduced demand for low-skilled workers.... Compulsory

unionism and militant union tactics were encouraged under a series of laws.... While "millions of jobs" were created in the government during the 1930s, private-sector jobs were destroyed.[4]

How do federal jobs programs break the back of the economy? Government jobs are funded by the private sector through taxation. One unintended consequence of public-employment programs is that resources are drained from the private sector, which then has a diminished amount of its profits available to invest in business expansion and job creation.

God's wisdom tells us that we can't spend tomorrow's money today and be prosperous in the long run. It's absolute truth. We can delay the impact for the short term, but we'll never outrun it.

We don't defy the law of gravity; we discover it. We can put on a parachute or strap on a hang glider to soften gravity's impact, but we cannot change its reality.

The fixed economic laws governing the consequences of overspending caught up to President Roosevelt. America suffered a second depression *within* the Great Depression. If you compare and contrast US history with that of other nations, we had the *Great* Depression while the world had a depression. The Dow Jones Average fell 50 percent as the Second New Deal picked up speed. Roosevelt was trying to reverse the economic law that spending tomorrow's money today cannot heal chronic economic illness.

Edwards explains:

Real output only regained its 1929 level in 1936, but then output plunged again in 1938. The unemployment rate stayed persistently high at more than 14 percent for 10 years (1931 to 1940). By contrast, the economy recovered rapidly after a sharp contraction in 1921. Real output fell 9 percent in 1921 and unemployment rose to 11.7 percent. But the economy bounced back with output recovering all its lost ground in 1922. Unemployment fell to 6.7 percent in 1922 and 2.4

percent in 1923. The secret to the quick recovery was that the government generally stood aside and let the market recover by itself....

By contrast, government policies in the 1930s prevented the U.S. economy from recovering.[5]

Not only did the ailing Dow Jones fall, it stayed at almost record lows for more than twenty-five years. The higher FDR's deficit spending rose and the more he attempted to regulate the level of prices and wages, the higher the unemployment rate remained. The honest diagnosis? The federal government, by continuing a failed policy of overspending, was draining wealth from the private sector. Ironically, this was a period when the private sector most desperately needed the use of all its remaining wealth to grow business and make the private investments that would enable the economy to recover.

Roosevelt could have fueled genuine economic growth by reducing federal spending and allowing the market to right itself. Instead, he chose to let the federal government continue to live far beyond its means.

One thing history does show clearly is that the United States, after more than a decade, pulled out of the Great Depression. So what was it that reversed the decline? Standard history textbooks credit the nationwide mobilization of manufacturing, commodities production, energy production, technology development, and research and development—all of which were maximized to supply the war effort. But this conclusion bears a closer look. Before accepting the conventional doctrine that our entry into World War II brought America out of the Great Depression, remember that a war requires even higher levels of deficit spending. While it's true that the demand for goods increases dramatically, the demand was fueled by government consumption by the armed forces. Wars don't fix economies; they consume from economies—shifting the production of wealth away from the private sector and funneling it into the war effort.

The truth about the United States' recovery can be found as America began *producing* again! The Great Depression cut the fat throughout much of American business and industry. It allowed many of the "booms" that were not backed by solid business practices, good management, adequate capital, and needed products to go bust. Those "busts" allowed the free market to reassess sound, long-term areas of investment and to begin the march toward lasting recovery.

New sectors of productive activity began to sprout. Nonproductive industry had been eliminated and now productive industries were being born. A renewed era of American ingenuity was able to overcome the consumption of resources during World War II.

The final skirmish that beat back the waste and deficit spending of the New Deal was a knock-out blow that originated with four Jewish butchers.

Four Butchers and a Policy Maker

The Schechter brothers ran kosher butcher shops in Brooklyn in the 1930's.... Their small business was about to become the key to stopping government intervention and releasing the free enterprise system again.... One of Roosevelt's early New Deal initiatives was the National Recovery Administration and was designed to stop competition—under the belief that too much competition was keeping prices on products too low. The New Deal's intention was higher prices to help business owners, but ultimately had the unintended consequence of setting up monopolies.... The Schechters' business was assaulted by or handcuffed by the "Code of Fair Competition for the Live Poultry Industry of the Metropolitan Area in and About the City of New York." The code prohibited "straight killing" which meant that customers could buy a whole chicken, but were not allowed to select particular birds of their choice (known as straight killing). These rules were not only anti-free enterprise, but in direct conflict with the Jewish community's Kashrut laws. Removing unhealthy animals from a group of animals was one of the core principles Rabbi's followed in keeping Kosher.... The Schechters refused to comply and were targeted by the NRA enforcement crew who inspected them often during the summer of 1934. The NRA forced them to tell customers that they were not allowed to follow their tradition and religious practice. The customer base was angry and the business was beginning to fail. They were taken to court and found guilty of sixty violations serving some jail time for daring to sell meat in a way the government deemed inappropriate.

...Their lawyer fought and appealed all the way to the Supreme Court. The Roosevelt Administration welcomed the opportunity to validate the New Deal in the highest court in the land.... [But] the Supreme Court stripped the NRA of its power declaring—in a unanimous decision—that it was unconstitutional. This was the first of several blows to the New Deal by the court.[6]

Despite all the revisionist history, common sense tells us that what got us out of the Great Depression is what makes any economy work: production in the private sector. Yet today, politicians and economists are responding to the economic meltdown of 2008 with the failed policies of the past. They continue to borrow more money and charge it to future taxpayers.

A recovery is not sustainable unless it is based on the essentials of producing, profiting, saving, and investing. The false recovery following 2008 was based on consuming, borrowing, and inflating.

The Dow Jones Average began rising after the Great Recession of 2008 because the dollar was worth less! It takes more devalued dollars to buy the same stock. As the federal government prints more currency, it keeps stocks afloat—for a while. But sadly, just as the false recovery of the New Deal had to come crashing down, today's inflated currency is creating a future tidal wave of consequences that may outweigh the damage caused by the Great Depression. (We'll talk more about inflation in a later chapter.)

7

What Would God Say to FDR About Budgeting?

Never substitute borrowing for a sound,
sustainable financial policy

The history lesson provided by Franklin Delano Roosevelt's New Deal policies shows the necessity of a realistic federal budget. A sustainable fiscal policy is based on a budget that assures that the revenue coming in annually exceeds the amount of annual federal expenditures.

The tendency to get overextended financially is a struggle for individuals just as much as it is for federal policy makers. Jesus pointed out what lures us into this trap: wanting more than we can afford. He warned, "Take heed and beware of covetousness" (Luke 12:15). On a practical level, whether it's members of Congress debating an appropriations bill or a family seeking ways to get out of debt, a budget is the key to success.

Budgeting to a Vision

The lack of budgeting, whether as a nation, a family, or an individual, has definite moral consequences. Spending money you don't have is not just irresponsible; it is unjust because it creates unfair burdens on others. Debt steals a family's financial security and peace of mind. Deficit spending guarantees a heavy tax burden on future taxpayers—those who do not benefit from today's government largesse.

Godonomics teaches that the most important thing we can do, whether in times of plenty or times of need, is learn to budget. A budget governs spending decisions, rather than leaving those decisions up to political expediency or, in the case of individuals, a driving desire to buy and possess more than we can afford.

Following are two passages from the Bible that speak to the importance of budgeting. God told the prophet Habakkuk to write out what the future holds, so God's people could plan and act accordingly. "Write the vision and make it plain on tablets, that he may run who reads it" (Habakkuk 2:2). Wisdom requires that we plan now for future eventualities so we won't be caught unprepared. This applies to our finances just as it applies to all major areas of life.

Solomon tells us to learn from ants, who work hard in the present so they will be well provisioned in the future. "Go to the ant, you sluggard! Consider her ways and be wise, which, having no captain, overseer or ruler, provides her supplies in the summer, and gathers her food in the harvest" (Proverbs 6:6–8).

R. C. Sproul Jr. put it this way in his book *Biblical Economics:* "How do we find freedom again? As individuals and families, it is simple enough. We do not follow the path to poverty, consuming more than we produce. Instead we follow the path to prosperity, producing more than we consume. Don't sell tomorrow's labor for today's consumption!"[1]

We must budget, saving back some money today for tomorrow's giving, investing, and spending. Additionally, we must budget and plan, preparing for tomorrow's unexpected problems—as Habakkuk shows us.

Budgeting for the Unexpected

The world we live in does not operate according to God's original blueprint. Natural disasters, the unwise acts of others, and our own covetousness are just the beginning of the problems. Because this world is filled with evil, the Bible teaches us to diversify our savings. "Give a serving to seven, and also to eight, for you do not know what evil will be on the earth" (Ecclesiastes 11:2). The writer is advising readers to diversify their savings and investments in seven or eight different places. The reason for diversifying is that we do not "know what evil will be on the earth."

My wife and I felt the sting of this firsthand in 2009. A few months after holding our newborn, adopted son Quinn in our arms, bad news was delivered. I was heading out to coach our son Javan's soccer game. I asked my wife for a quick summary of Quinn's doctor appointment. I assumed the answer would be, "Great, everything is on track!"

My eyes caught hers, and I knew something was wrong. As I watched clouds gathering behind my wife's tear-filled eyes, I sat down and tried to prepare myself for the news.

"The doctor says Quinn has a condition called ONH. His optic nerve is underdeveloped. The doctor says he may never see anything and that it is incurable. Chad, the doctor says Quinn is blind."

I tried to process the words *incurable* and *blind* in relation to my son. I was simultaneously in denial, anger, and bargaining mode. My mind raced with thoughts like, *We adopted him. We did the right thing! Our son doesn't deserve this. I wonder if I can teach my son how to overcome the teasing of other children.*

I wondered if I could lead my family through what felt like a kick in the teeth. My wife and I cried. We prayed. I called my parents in tears to share the news. My mom and dad both picked up the phone. They listened for a while and then my mom said, "Chad, God will give you the strength and wisdom you need. You will rise to the occasion. God will give you whatever you need to be the father Quinn needs you to be. God will use this in a powerful way."

My parents were instilling in me the courage to face the reality that the writer of Ecclesiastes had warned about. We do not know "what evil will be on the earth." But we have hope. If God could turn the tragedy of a wooden cross into a glorious path to forgiveness, then I was confident that He could provide both emotionally and financially for my new son's physical condition as well.

Budgeting for the unexpected means we should not put all our eggs in one basket. When tragedy strikes one area, diversification allows the possibility that other areas will remain untouched.

In the New Testament, James admonished his readers not to budget by presuming upon tomorrow's certainty. "Come now, you who say, 'Today or tomorrow we will go to such and such a city, spend a year there, buy and sell, and make a profit'; whereas you do not know what will happen tomorrow" (James 4:13–14).

It is foolhardy to assume that tomorrow will never bring a health crisis, a financial reversal, or some other major disruption of our plans. This is the problem of leveraging all our spending on the assumption we will always have our current job. If history tells us anything, it's that we can be certain only about uncertainty. In fact, Jesus made it clear that life will not be a continuous smooth path: "In the world you will have tribulation" (John 16:33).

President Roosevelt and the administrations that followed kept spending more money than was in the federal treasury. They bet on constant years of plenty and, beyond that, did not even maintain the revenues that were earmarked for predetermined future expenditures. Worker and employer contributions to the Social Security fund, for instance, were not protected. Instead, they were tapped into for other programs.

When the Social Security Act was passed in the 1930s, the ratio of active wage earners to retirees who were eligible to draw benefits was favorable to a financially solvent fund. However, baby boomers are now retiring in unprecedented numbers at a time when a diminished birth rate has produced far fewer American workers. With fewer employees paying into the system and the baby boom becoming a retirement boom, the assumptions made when the Social Security system was established are now proven to be deeply flawed.

We find wisdom for life, as well as a guideline for sound government policy, in the words of James: "You do not know what will happen tomorrow" (James 4:14).

8

What Would God Say to FDR About Liberty?

Never exchange freedom for perceived security

In a time of national crisis, a natural tendency is to want to get back to normal as quickly as possible. We long to return to a sense of normalcy and to regain a sense of security. But while these desires are understandable, they are not a reliable basis for sound decision making.

The Bible gives us detailed warnings about the consequences for turning to government—rather than God—for our security. In the same vein, it warns us about giving up liberty in exchange for perceived security.

It was a time of national crisis in Israel, as foreign nations posed a constant threat. In response to the warring Philistines, the Israelites were contemplating a new type of government. Neighboring nations had kings, and the Israelites felt that a king would bring them more security. So they asked the prophet Samuel to petition God for a king.

God had been teaching them for years about the importance of trusting Him as their King. He revealed the value of using His wisdom to build a nation. He said, "Trust Me to give you liberty. Trust Me to give you wisdom. I will make you prosperous. You will be a light in the darkness."

Israel could choose to trust God in spite of the uncertainty of freedom, or the people could move forward with a new, intrusive government ruled by a human king. The Israelites had tried judges and prophets. Now they acted on their longing for a sense of normalcy and security, concluding that an earthly king would fix their problems.

Then all the elders of Israel gathered together and came to Samuel at Ramah, and said to him, "Look, you are old, and your sons do not walk in your ways. Now make us a king to judge us like all the nations."

But the thing displeased Samuel when they said, "Give us a king to judge us." (1 Samuel 8:4–6)

Samuel had seen foreign kings steal liberty, prosperity, and the opportunity for generosity from their people for decades. Still, he took the Israelites' request to God.

So Samuel prayed to the LORD.

And the LORD said to Samuel,… "They have not rejected you, but they have rejected Me, that I should not reign over them.…

"However, you shall solemnly forewarn them, and show them the behavior of the king who will reign over them." (1 Samuel 8:6–7, 9)

History has shown that kings, tyrants, and dictators take from the people. They take away liberty, and they take away the citizens' wealth and possessions (see 1 Samuel 8:11–17).

The producers would be taxed heavily, both financially and in human terms. A king would take their sons and daughters to work for the government, to manufacture weapons, and to serve in other capacities for the king. God warned the people of Israel not to trade their liberty for perceived security under the rule of an earthly king.

As you know from reading the history of Israel, the people demanded a king anyway.

The Forgotten Man

Amity Shlaes has noted that an almost identical pattern has played out again and again throughout history. She describes this principle as "The Forgotten

Man." It involves the loss of freedom on the part of the many, the exercise of power by a few, and an attempt to provide help to those who need it.[1]

Let's say person A is in need. Person B is not a producer in the economy and has no self-derived assets, but person C is a producer and has extra. What should be done to help person A? We could have person C choose to give generously to help person A. But what if person C does not choose to be generous in that way? How will help be arranged for person A?

In this illustration, person B is a government that has the power to move money around but is not a producer in the economy. The government (person B) sees that person A is in need, so person B forces person C to give up a portion of his money to assist person A. The money is channeled through person B (the government), who keeps a portion of person C's mandated contribution as an administrative fee and to use in financing other projects. The one who needed help, person A, received help, but at the expense of person C. It came about only through the coercive efforts of person B, resulting in a loss of liberty for person C.

So who is the forgotten man? It's not person A; it is person C.

In biblical times, the king saw himself as person A—deeply in need of assets contributed by all the person Cs (the peasants, farmers, merchants, and others). The king needed financial assistance to pay for his army and a host of building projects. In fact, the king's military (person B) supplied the leverage to coerce tax payments from the person Cs.

This is why Christ-followers historically have favored a smaller and less intrusive government. They know that at the heart of all human beings is a selfish spirit. If we don't limit the size and power of government, it will become a self-serving mercenary force that takes from one group to give to another.

This is true of both major political parties in America. Democrats in power favor labor unions (person As), which benefit from the government's (person Bs) power to force corporations (person Cs) to give concessions and additional benefits to unions (person As). Republicans in power favor corporations (person As) and use the power of government (person Bs) to coerce taxpayers (person Cs) into bailing out failing corporations that are suffering the consequences of their own flawed business decisions. Until a government's power is restricted, this destructive dance will never end.

Every few years we hear about campaign-finance reform. The assumption is that legislation needs to be adopted that would keep people from influencing the outcome of elections by making large financial donations to certain candidates and political causes.

But on a practical level, the theory behind campaign-finance reform is flawed. First, it removes the freedom of individuals to support in a material way the causes and candidates they believe in. Second, we all know that government is controlled by campaign donors. So, third, what are the chances that campaign-finance legislation would be completely nonpartisan in the way donors and donations are restricted? It is highly likely that the party in power would design a law that favors donors who support candidates and causes sympathetic to its own party while limiting the ability of donors to other parties to work within the law.

The only way to free ourselves from escalating government coercion is to limit the government's power. If the government is allowed by law to perform only a handful of duties—such as protecting the nation's borders, negotiating international treaties, managing foreign policy, and assuring justice in the courts—then the potential for abuses is greatly reduced. The Constitution and the Bill of Rights spell out the legal scope of the federal government. And even the power to punish convicted criminals and administer justice has restraints, such as protecting citizens against delayed trials and being tried twice for the same crime, and the outlawing of cruel and unusual punishment (in the Fourth through Eighth Amendments).

With a federal government that is limited to a few specific areas of responsibility, it would be irrelevant how much campaign money comes from what groups. Neither unions nor corporations could pay the government to legislate favorable treatment at the expense of others. A limited government would pass laws that apply equally to all citizens and all sectors of society and the economy.

No longer would one set of laws apply to ordinary citizens while the nation's leaders are allowed to operate under a different, more favorable set of rules and regulations. We would get back to the idea that justice is blind.

Our nation's founders knew that self-interest and the lure of power among the nation's leaders would present a dangerous challenge to a democratic society. That is why they limited the power of the federal government through decentralizing authority into three branches, and through a careful system of checks and balances. The Tenth Amendment to the United States Constitution states, "The powers not delegated to the United States by the Constitution, nor prohibited by it to the States, are reserved to the States respectively, or to the people."[2]

This amendment has been virtually ignored during the past hundred years. However, it is designed to keep the federal government from being employed in the cause of any group of citizens, not to mention unions, industry, agriculture, mining, insurance, healthcare, Wall Street—any type of interest group. This is not to say that state governments are somehow immune to waste, corruption, and the coercion of citizens. But the founders knew that the levels of government that are closer to the people find it far more difficult to escape accountability for their policies and actions.

The Bible notes that God set up governments to punish evildoers: those who lie, steal, murder, and infringe on the rights of others. Paul noted that one of the legitimate roles of government is the punishing of evil.

Let every soul be subject to the governing authorities. For there is no authority except from God, and the authorities that exist are appointed by God. Therefore whoever resists the authority resists the ordinance of God, and those who resist will bring judgment on themselves. For rulers are not a terror to good works, but to evil. Do you want to be unafraid of the authority? Do what is good, and you will have praise from the same. For he is God's minister to you for good. But if you do evil, be afraid; for he does not bear the sword in vain; for he is God's minister, an avenger to execute wrath on him who practices evil. Therefore you must be subject, not only because of wrath but also for conscience' sake. (Romans 13:1–5)

When government is working properly, it executes wrath on those who practice evil.

An interesting follow-up to God's warnings against trading His rule for that of an earthly king comes in the book of Deuteronomy. God knew the people would not heed His warnings against sacrificing their freedom in exchange for having a king, so He provided a game plan in which the king was subject to laws just as the people were. God told Israel that once their king was anointed, the king was to read daily the Law of God and remind himself that he was subject to God's rule. God told the kings, starting with Saul, to read the Law "all the days of his life" that "his heart may not be lifted above his brethren" (Deuteronomy 17:19–20).

God knew a king would be tempted to think he was above the Law. The same is true today. Rulers operate as if they exist on a different level, above the laws that apply to the citizens. But God's requirement for rulers in Deuteronomy 17 established the basis for what became known later as a republic. The foundation of a real republic is that even the top official in a government—no matter what title the ruler has—is subject to a system of law that is applied fairly and evenly to everyone. The government's role is to protect the liberty, life, and property of its citizens by punishing evil, enforcing contracts, and ensuring equal access to a fair hearing under the law.

Also notice something that God prohibited kings from doing. A king was not to multiply riches for himself (see Deuteronomy 17:17). This was a necessary prohibition, since rulers and public servants, due to their positions, face the temptation to use their influence as a way to enrich themselves with the public's money.

The people of Israel longed for a king who would not steal their liberty or divert their prosperity into the king's treasury. They dreamed of a king who would give them more freedom, not less. They needed someone to whom they could fully surrender with complete security and peace.

Saul, the first king of Israel, failed on all counts. David, who ascended to the throne next, is considered the greatest of Israel's kings, but he was still vulnerable to his overwhelming passions and shortsighted reliance on expediency. Solomon built the glorious temple in Jerusalem but allowed his devotion to God to be compromised by pagan influences. And after Solomon, the kingdom was divided, and Israel lost her glory.

However, God remained faithful and answered Israel's prayers! King Jesus came to earth in the most humble of circumstances. When He entered Jerusalem at the beginning of the week leading up to His crucifixion, He did not ride into the city on the back of a beautiful stallion like most kings. Jesus came as a humble, others-focused King. While other kings would sacrifice their servants for the sake of their kingdom, this King sacrificed His life for the sake of His servants! What kind of King is this?

Only Christ promises us a treasure that is kept where it will never tarnish. When He becomes your security, you find peace. When you make Jesus your King, you can trust Him with your decisions, your plans, your future, your very life. You can rest assured that this King will guide you with His wisdom, no matter what lies ahead of you. A government cannot save you. But Jesus the King already has, and you can base your security on His rule in your life.

PART 5

If God Were Talking to Former Fed Chief Alan Greenspan

What Would God Say to Alan Greenspan About the Money Supply?

What a sound currency does to help the poor

God would have much to say to Alan Greenspan, the former Federal Reserve chairman who served for eighteen years, beginning in the second term of President Ronald Reagan.[1]

The Federal Reserve System controls the US banking system. This privately owned bank has more influence over the nation's economy and our money than any other single entity in America. Before we dig into how the Fed works, let's face the hard truth that money has the power to deceive us. It has the power of illusion. I've been an illusionist since I was ten years old. A few years ago, I called upon my talent in this area to help my kids understand money's deceptive power.

I had sold a boat several years earlier for three thousand dollars. I brought the hundred-dollar bills into our living room and spread them out on the coffee table. My kids had never seen so much money. I wanted to take advantage of their fascination with this much cash appearing there in front of them. "Money is important," I said, "but money can take our hearts away from God."

We talked about the ways that money can be used for good, but how the love of money causes problems. "In fact," I said, "I'm so concerned that money may one day take your heart away from God, we're going to burn this three thousand dollars. It will remind us that God is more important than cash."

I put the thirty hundred-dollar bills into a paper bag. The kids began protesting. They couldn't believe I was going through with this insanity.

"Dad, we get the point," they insisted.

We went outside to the fire pit, where I set the paper bag on top of a pile of wood. We poured kerosene over the bag and took out matches. Javan and Sierra tried to intervene one last time. "Dad, you don't have to do this!"

"Nope, we need to make sure money hasn't deceived us. If we burn it, it can't take the place of things that really matter."

I lit a match and tossed it onto the bag, igniting a burst of flames. "Dad, OK," my kids said. "Can we stop now? Could we save at least some of the money?"

The bag disintegrated into ashes. My children were dumbfounded. "Dad," they asked, "why did you do that?"

Remember, I'm an illusionist. On our way outside, I switched the bag containing three thousand genuine dollars with an identical bag filled with Monopoly money.

The kids will never forget that episode. They know that anything that comes between our hearts and God needs to be radically dealt with. We must realign our hearts and lives again and again, making sure God is our priority.

The Value of Money

God would most certainly talk to Alan Greenspan about illusions. Likewise, if we want to experience liberty, prosperity, and generosity, we have to understand three illusions: the illusion of value, the illusion of abundance, and the illusion of generosity. Remember, Godonomics is about producing, which leads to profiting. Profiting leads to saving, and savings allow us to give, invest, and spend.

Unfortunately, the US economy is currently built on consuming rather than producing. As we have seen, Keynesian economics enriches the government in one of three ways: borrowing from other nations, taxing the citizens (the producers), or increasing the money supply, which means inflating the currency.

The devaluation of the dollar by the government's printing of more currency creates the illusion of a healthier economy while allowing the nation to avoid budgeting. This economic approach, popular during the years when Alan Greenspan was Fed chief, points to a tempting deadly illusion, the illusion of value.

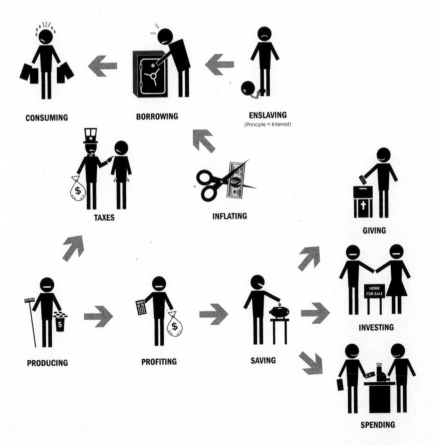

The Illusion of Value

The Old Testament prophet Micah observed those who were exploiting and cheating the poor. They were powerful people who made use of dishonest scales. Speaking for God, the prophet condemned them, saying, "Shall I acquit a man with dishonest scales, with a bag of false weights?" (Micah 6:11, NIV).

In Micah's time a buyer would make purchases using silver or gold coins. When it came time to buy a sheep, for instance, a standardized weight equal to the value of the sheep would be placed on a scale to match the correct amount of silver or gold due. The standardized weight was set on one side of the scale while the buyer's coins were set on the other side. When the scale balanced, both parties knew the proper amount had been given in exchange for the livestock.

Let's say the standardized weight for the price of a sheep was one ounce. A seller would set a one-ounce weight on one side of the scale, and the buyer would place coins on the other side until the scale was balanced. This weighing system allowed for honest and fair transactions.

But what if you were dealing with a sheep broker who gave only the illusion of fair value? A dishonest businessman would add a little extra weight to his "standardized" ounce. Tampering with the weight would result in more than one ounce of coins being required for the purchase of a sheep—cheating the buyer and unfairly padding the seller's profits. What's more, by falsifying the counterweight, the seller devalued the buyer's money. Since a true ounce of coins now had less buying power when balanced against a false weight, the buyer needed to hand over more money to purchase a sheep.

The buyer walked away with a sheep valued at one ounce of coins, but the seller banked more than one ounce of coins. The buyer's money had been devalued.

God's words spoken through Micah apply to the economic policies of Alan Greenspan. Greenspan headed the Federal Reserve until he passed the baton to Ben Bernanke during the George W. Bush administration. What would God say to Fed chiefs Greenspan and Bernanke? He would surely ask them, "Why are you using dishonest scales? How can you deliberately hurt the economy, and harm the poor, by devaluing the dollar?"

Before we can understand how the devaluing of currency takes place, we have to understand what gives value to a nation's currency. Until 1971, the value of the dollar was determined by linking it to a commodity. The standard in the United States was gold, until President Richard Nixon decided to sever the link between the precious metal and America's currency. Countries print money because it is much more convenient to carry and use. But in the United States, prior to 1971, you could trade dollars for a corresponding standardized weight of gold. This system, referred to as "the gold standard," accomplished several goals.

First, because the value of the dollar was tied to a commodity, the federal government could not simply print more money—unless a corresponding amount of gold had been added to the national treasury. This forced lawmakers to settle on a national budget that reflected the existing money supply. The gold standard restricted the amount of money that could be printed and put into circulation.

However, President Woodrow Wilson felt that the gold standard was unnecessarily restrictive. He began to move the country away from the gold standard in 1913. Breaking the dollar's direct link to gold was, he assured, not a risk, since the government would not print so many dollars that it would devalue the currency.

That, of course, is not what happened. When the government prints extra dollars, each individual dollar loses some of its value. Think of a dollar like a block of wood measuring four inches by four inches by eight inches. Glue a dollar bill onto the wood. What you have now is a dollar that has weight—the weight of an eight-inch length of a four-by-four.

When the Federal Reserve decides to print more currency, it pushes the value of the current dollars through a spinning saw blade. Imagine the

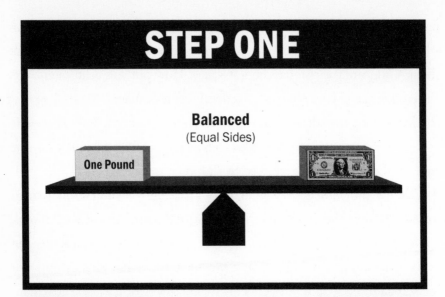

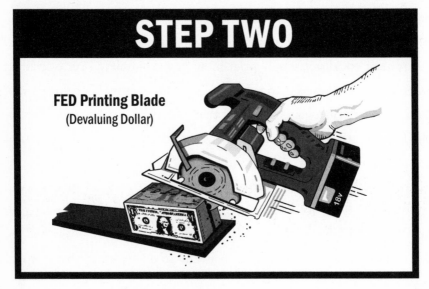

one-dollar block of wood being pushed through a table saw. There are now two "dollars" instead of one, but each one is only half as thick, and thus has only half as much purchasing power. We have more money in circulation, because of the increase in the quantity of dollars. The bad news is that each of the new dollars is worth less.

The act of increasing the supply of currency in circulation is that new dollars do not match the "weight" of dollars prior to the increase in the money supply. When compared to the standard value of one old dollar, a new dollar will fall short. However, it will still be called a "dollar," and the pretense is that it still is, in fact, equal to one dollar.

As illustrated, the only way to match the previous, accepted value of one old dollar is to put more than one of the new dollars on the scale. It now takes more than one new dollar to match the weight of what, prior to this, had been the accepted value of a dollar.

The buying power of these dollars was split down the middle. What are the consequences of spending less-valuable dollars? For the seller, prices go up. But on the negative side, for the buyer, the same commodity or service now costs more. The selling price of your house went up, which might seem to be an advantage. Yet the price of the house you want to buy also increased. The value of your stocks is rising, but filling your car with gas now costs a lot more.

Things now cost more not because the intrinsic value or worth of groceries, clothing, rent, or repairs to your automobile went up; it's because your dollars are worth less. It now takes more of your less-valuable dollars to make the same purchases you used to make.

Since 1913, the US dollar has lost 85 to 97 percent of its value. This hurts the entire economy, and it especially hurts the poor. As the printing-press saw blade spins, the prices for necessities go up. The more prices go up, the more money the government needs to print. The cycle continues. This is a way of stealing from the public without admitting it. Just as John Maynard Keynes conceded by quoting Vladimir Lenin, the government is able to steal the citizens' prosperity right out from under their noses: "The best way to destroy the capitalist system is to debauch the currency. By a continuing process of inflation, governments can confiscate, secretly and unobserved, an important part of the wealth of their citizens."[2]

This is why dishonest scales are an abomination to the Lord. A just weight or standardized weight in our monetary system ensures a consistent value. It is what we call "sound money." God delights in consistent, sound money because He knows the benefits it provides to a nation. Sound money reflects honesty and integrity in transactions, and God has a lot to say about that.

> You shall do no injustice in judgment, in measurement of length, weight, or volume. You shall have honest scales, honest weights, an honest ephah.... I am the LORD your God, who brought you out of the land of Egypt. (Leviticus 19:35–36)

> You shall not have in your bag differing weights, a heavy and a light. You shall not have in your house differing measures, a large and a small. You shall have a perfect and just weight, a perfect and just measure, that your days may be lengthened in the land which the LORD your God is giving you. For all who do such things, all who behave unrighteously, are an abomination to the LORD your God. (Deuteronomy 25:13–16)

If you have never taken a child to a Chuck E. Cheese's, you need to do it. It's educational for a parent, although it's a hard lesson.

You and your kids enter the arcade restaurant and purchase twenty dollars' worth of tokens. As your kids spend their tokens and win certain games, they collect tickets. At the end of the night, the tickets are counted and used by the children to purchase toys at the toy counter.

The kids are thrilled when they take more than 1,700 points in children's currency to the toy counter. Their eyes gleam with hopes of trading for some real treasures. The prize wall above the counter is covered with iPods and giant stuffed animals. The kids have played hard in hopes of earning enough tickets to purchase an expensive prize.

But when the employee at the toy counter totals up the value of their currency, it turns out the tickets don't have the buying power the kids had expected. It takes 500 points just to purchase a Blow Pop. It takes 1,000 points to earn a Chinese handcuff. The iPods and giant stuffed bears cost more than 900,000 points! After all the excitement, hard work, and hype, the kids are sorely disappointed.

As the parent, you can see that the twenty dollars you spent on game tokens were devalued by the end of the evening, purchasing toys that would cost less than a dollar and a half at any Dollar Store. So what happened? The people in charge of the currency (the issuer, Chuck E. Cheese's) had tinkered with the value of the tickets that are issued for winning certain games. Even after you take into account that your kids' enjoyment of playing games had some value, something about the system seems out of proportion.

The federal government's central planning bears more than a little similarity to an evening at Chuck E. Cheese's. The dollar lost as much as 97 percent of its value over the past hundred years. The result? An ice-cream cone that cost twenty-six cents when my grandfather drove me to McDonalds in 1978 now costs more than a dollar. Is the ice cream that much more valuable? No, and the fact is, the real price of the ice-cream cone has not risen astronomically. It's the result of dollars and cents being worth less.

Inflation is the most insidious tax imposed upon the American people.

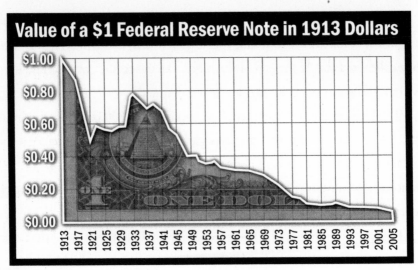

Source: U.S. Bureau of Labor Statistics

The fact that we don't see this tax as an amount that is withheld from our paychecks does not shelter us from feeling the weight of its impact.

The chart above tracks the erosion of the value of the US dollar since 1913. Imagine all the financial giving you could engage in and all the vacations you could go on if suddenly every five-dollar bill in your wallet changed into a hundred-dollar note. That's what it would feel like if inflation had not eroded the value of your money. You can go to the US government's website and test it out. Enter a dollar amount and a year, and request its current worth. Let's say you bought a car in 1980 for $10,000. How much would that be in today's dollars? The answer is $26,509. A $10,000 car today will cost you $26,509! Go to http://data.bls.gov/cgi-bin/cpicalc.pl, or Google "government inflation calculator." The federal government has the brass to tell you how much it has devalued your currency.

How we define *inflation* is a key factor in this debate. The two leading schools of economic thought are Austrian economics and Keynesian economics. A Keynesian defines inflation as "prices going up." An Austrian economist defines inflation as "increasing the money supply"—which results in prices going up in the near future.

While a Keynesian thinks inflation is *defined* by rising prices, Austrian economists know that inflation *leads* to rising prices. Because the dollar is becoming worth less, prices will soon go up because it will take more of your less-valuable dollars to buy the same items.

What would God say to Alan Greenspan and the Federal Reserve? "Stop the presses!" Why? Because in the name of printing money for important government programs that help the poor, as well as military spending, farm subsidies, and a smorgasbord of other government brainstorms, some more legitimate than others, the poor now have even less than before when you recalculate the value of their limited financial resources. When the US dollar is devalued, it hurts the poor most of all. It is an abomination to God when a nation legitimizes imbalanced weights. "Diverse weights are an abomination to the LORD, and dishonest scales are not good" (Proverbs 20:23).

The Illusion of an Economic "Bubble"

The illusion of value gets even more complicated. You often hear about "bubbles" in the economy. The Housing Bubble serves as an apt illustration. What is your home worth? You might have an appraisal from 2007 that set the value at $175,000. If your home is really worth that amount, then why, if you had tried to sell it in 2009, would the selling price have been far less than that amount?

The value of a house or a used car or a collection of rare books is the amount that a buyer is willing to pay. The marketplace decides value, which helps explain the illusion of the Housing Bubble.

The law of supply and demand is one of the basic principles of capitalism. The way to attract a larger pool of potential buyers for your home is to increase the supply of buyers who meet a standard of eligibility. If you have more buyers out looking for a home, the price of homes will rise due to increased competition from a larger pool of customers. Sellers receive more offers and, as a result, stand to get higher prices for their homes.

The Federal Reserve increases the number of buyers in two ways: by lowering interest rates on home loans, and by requiring banks to approve high-risk loans to potential buyers. First, let's look at the manipulation of interest rates.

With lower interest rates, a potential buyer's monthly payment, as well as the amount she will pay over the term of the mortgage, is lower than before. By regulating the rate of interest, rather than letting the natural effect of supply and demand determine the market value of a home, a forced lower interest rate allows more buyers to qualify for loans.

When this happens, you have people shopping for homes who have not saved enough of a down payment and whose incomes—when held to a reasonable standard—do not qualify for so high a mortgage. However, they are deemed to be qualified nonetheless. Thus, the housing market suddenly has a far greater number of "qualified" buyers.

This has an immediate short-term benefit. When a flood of new buyers rush into the housing market, housing prices balloon upward. The Housing Bubble has begun to grow.

The second way the government increases the number of buyers is through government regulation that requires banks to make high-risk loans to buyers who aren't qualified. When this policy was instituted, the government again was messing with the law of supply and demand, in order to drive up the number of buyers. For years, government programs such as Fannie Mae (the Federal National Mortgage Association) threatened banks and lenders if they did not issue enough mortgages. This led to loan approvals for buyers with bad credit and/or with insufficient down payments. Thus, people who should have continued to rent while they saved up larger down payments were approved for mortgage loans. The short-term "illusion of value" was that there were more seemingly qualified buyers on the market, which drove up housing prices.

Home prices escalated because of devalued dollars paired with this larger supply of home buyers.

While Alan Greenspan and the Fed kept interest rates low, Americans were assured that real estate was a can't-miss investment. It was easy to believe the illusion that prices would continue to rise year after year. These were the "inflate-the-bubble" years. But eventually the housing market began to right itself.

When you continue to force air into a balloon or bubble, it will burst. In time, the Housing Bubble exploded. (And let's not overlook the contributions made by corporate corruption. The financial sector, after approving high-risk loans, was repackaging the debt and selling it to get-rich-quick buyers.)

Who is really to blame for all of this? Everyone involved. Buyers, sellers, politicians, banks, and the financial sector at large all violated the Golden Rule and common sense, producing the economic meltdown of 2008. This is why Godonomics teaches nonpartisan principles. These laws of economic reality apply to everyone equally.

The year 2008 brought the collapse of the Housing Bubble and falling prices through a process of deflation. While it's painful to see your home now valued at less than you paid for it, deflation can help the economy. As housing prices drop, the prices of other commodities go down as well. Deflation makes food, housing, and energy cheaper. It also rewards savers who have been waiting until prices come down to make wise purchases. The economy is stimulated because more people can now afford to buy the lower-priced homes. Business profits increase as sales volumes increase. Instead of making a 10 percent profit on a hundred units sold, they make a 5 percent profit on three hundred units sold. It is painful to go through an overpriced economy falling back to reality, reconnecting prices to actual worth. But the alternative is far worse, for continued inflation only produces a much bigger explosion in the end.

As prices began to deflate during 2008 and 2009, the government said, "Don't worry! We're going to 'catch' deflating prices by inflating the currency. We'll stop your house's price from settling all the way back to where the market says it should be by printing more money." Once again, big government intervening in the natural supply-and-demand forces of the market makes things worse. It becomes increasingly difficult to determine what real value is because the Fed keeps messing with the weights. The whole thing is an illusion!

It's time for something better. It's time for wise, sound monetary policy and reliable currency. It's time for the illusion to stop.

The books of Deuteronomy and Proverbs show a direct connection between sound money and honoring the poor and needy (see Deuteronomy 25:15 and Proverbs 14:31). If you weigh and measure things properly, the Lord will let you enjoy a long life in the land.

When God gave the Law to Moses, it was a legal structure that was to be applied to all people equally, a universal moral law that would protect and benefit an entire society. Though we live in a world of deception and illusion where up seems down and what seems right can lead to our destruction, our heavenly Father says, "Follow Me. Trust Me. Stay on the path I've set for you. Do not turn to the left or to the right."

In Luke 19:45–46, Jesus demonstrates God's anger at financial corruption when he drives out the buyers and sellers from the temple and says, "It is written, 'My house is a house of prayer,' but you have made it a 'den of thieves.'"

People would travel great distances to come to Jerusalem to sacrifice to God at the temple. God had instructed people to bring their best sheep to sacrifice. But before a visitor was allowed into the temple, his sacrificial offering had to undergo an inspection. The scribes and priests had set up an insidious way to devalue an out-of-towner's "currency." In those days, a person's currency included money (silver, gold, and Roman coinage) as well as property (sheep, cows). When a worshiper brought a sheep to the temple, a priest who was party to the corrupt system would declare it unworthy for sacrifice, but then buy it at half its value. The priest would then sell the person a "qualified" animal at twice the price.

Once the person left the area, a priest would take the just-purchased "unqualified" animal, approve it, and sell it to the next person for twice the price. When I visited the Temple Mount recently, I researched this unjust practice. A group called the Sadducees set up a monopoly with the help of the wicked King Herod and the Roman government. The Sadducees owned all the sheep in Bethlehem and declared that only Bethlehem sheep were qualified for sacrifice. They cheated the pilgrims coming to worship by charging exorbitant prices for sacrificial animals. I witnessed some of the weights and balances that were uncovered in a Sadducee home. They were decidedly inaccurate. They used this system of coercion and corruption to finance unbelievably lavish lifestyles.

This is what Jesus was angry about. The religious and political leaders were robbing the people by devaluing their property and then overcharging them through rising prices.

The Bible teaches the importance of sound money as a protection for everyone in a community and a nation. What we see going on today in the monetary policies of the Federal Reserve is just as wrong as the Sadducees' corrupt practices in cheating worshipers in ancient Jerusalem.

What Would God Say to Alan Greenspan About Greed?

Confronting the dangerous illusion of abundance

Why do people borrow money so they can consume more than they should? Why do they willingly enslave themselves to their creditors? The short answer is that they have been taken in by the illusion of abundance.

Jesus issued timely warnings: "Take heed and beware of covetousness, for one's life does not consist in the abundance of the things he possesses" (Luke 12:15). "Watch out! Be on your guard against all kinds of greed; a man's life does not consist in the abundance of his possessions" (Luke 12:15, NIV).

In my fifteen years of pastoral ministry, no one has ever come into my office and said, "I'm really struggling with greed. Can you help me deal with this?" Greed is like a termite. It's out of sight but boring deep into our hearts. It doesn't attract attention as it eats away at our ability to be generous. Jesus warned us to be on our guard, so we can assume we are already infested with greed. If you have trouble spotting it, here's what it looks like:

- **Hoarding**. This type of greed tends to find a home in the heart of conscientious, disciplined, organized people. It preys on a person's ability to diligently set aside savings, adding regularly to the total. Of course, this is something we should all be doing. However, greed in the life of a hoarder leads him to believe that he can't be generous with his money until he has set aside enough money to ensure a comfortable retirement. The hoarder is insecure about the future. His willingness to trust money rather than God with his future drives him to ignore the needs of other people. He feels his first responsibility is to amass enough assets to secure what he assumes will be a safe future. But a hoarder falls into the trap of using all his resources to benefit only one person: the hoarder.

- **Overspending**. This form of greed fits easily into the life of an impatient person. The overspender confuses needs with wants and, as a result, spends more than her income allows, thus leading to debt. She wants things now and is willing to use credit to avoid having to wait.

- **Comparison**. Greed feeds the competitive sense that it's imperative to match the lifestyle of someone else. It drives you to spend and keep on spending as a way to show that you are equal to a neighbor, friend, coworker, or relative. This form of greed is closely aligned with envy.

- **Entitlement**. Greed lies behind a feeling of entitlement, the sense that someone else owes you something. An entitled person believes a lie: "I don't have the money for it, so somebody else ought to buy it for me. After all, I deserve to have it—and without having to work for it." This face of greed always displays a lack of gratitude and often reveals anger. Entitlement sends people on a consuming binge.

It's easy to accept the mistaken idea that rich people are the greedy ones. But greed preys on everyone, no matter what their net-worth statement looks like. When you believe the lie that abundance comes from your possessions, you will find greed lurking in the shadows.

Peter Schiff, an Austrian-style economist, tells a parable that illustrates the arrogance of our consumer-driven economy. Imagine four castaways stranded on an island. Three are Asians and one is an American. As they devise ways to survive, they decide to divvy up jobs. A man from China is put in charge of gathering wood. A Japanese woman is given responsibility for fishing. Another Chinese man is sent out to do some hunting. As the jobs are dispersed, the American gives himself the job of eating. At the end of each day, the Asians gather at the campfire and watch the American eat. Luckily, he leaves enough food untouched so the Asians can keep their strength up. After all, they are the ones who will go out the following day to gather more food and fuel.

With time on his hands, the American developed a business: a tanning salon. He staked out an area on the beach and used it on a daily basis to keep up his tan. While the American sunned himself, he stayed alive by consuming products gathered and produced by the other refugees. His tanning business had only one customer: himself. But he explained that production is overrated. Consuming is necessary for a healthy economy. His service-industry business was vital.[1]

Sadly, most modern economists would agree that the consuming, suntanned American is vital to the island's economy. Without the American doing his part by consuming, the Asians' jobs (fishing, hunting, firewood gathering) would not be needed. The economy would collapse.

It's nonsense, of course. If the Asians would kick the American off the island, their quality of life would improve immediately. They would have more food to eat, and they would not have to watch the tanned American consume the fruits of their hard work. Without having to feed the nonproducer, they might use the freed-up time to travel farther in their food gathering, resulting in a more diverse diet. Or they could use the time to build a boat and enjoy sailing on the weekends.

The producers on the island don't need to be told that the American's belief in his indispensible role as a leading consumer is ridiculous, and it is arrogance and greed. America has bought the lie that a consumer economy is necessary and sustainable. The lie is destroying our nation's economy. The United States must confront the greed that drives overconsumption and return to production.

I don't know you, but I can guarantee that the illusion of abundance has taken root in your heart. In some way, greed influences your decisions, attitudes, assumptions, and actions. Greed is an expert at hiding, so trying to root it out on your own is useless. You'll need a partner to help with the investigation. Find a wise person you trust, and ask him or her, "Do you see greed in my life?"

It takes courage to do this, and a willingness to be humbled. The person, if he or she knows you well, is likely to say, "For years, you have defined your value by what you wear or how much money you've saved or the success of your investments or the house you live in." Greed is an illusion that enslaves us through the lie that we can find our identity in our possessions, savings, or quarterly results. Meanwhile, it keeps us from being generous.

The Illusion of Generosity

We don't struggle with spending or even, oddly, with sharing. The problem we face is that our first inclination is to spend and share so that it benefits *ourselves*. Jesus said our problem is that we prefer to be rich toward ourselves rather than toward God (see Luke 12:16–21, especially verse 21). When we

GIVING

PRODUCING   PROFITING   SAVING   INVESTING profit from the abundance of what God allows us to produce, we often do not even think to ask how we can generously and selflessly share the profit with others.

The illusion of generosity is closely tied to the illusion of abundance. In other words, greed plays a big role in it. A man in our church told me that he and his wife were excited about the work our church was doing. He mentioned that he had decided to start tithing. "We're tithing a hundred dollars a month to the church," he said. "We hope God will use it to impact a lot of people."

"That's awesome," I said, smiling inside. The man was a lawyer, and I knew he made a really good living. The word *tithe* means "10 percent." The excited lawyer had decided to give at a rate that reflected an annual salary of twelve thousand dollars.

He was not earning $12,000 a year, but still he was caught up in the illusion of generosity. This illusion causes us to redefine God's standards downward and then to feel proud about measuring up to our own impoverished standard. If the lawyer had been earning $240,000 per year, his "generous giving" would amount to one-half of one percent.

Help in the area of generosity is available if we're willing to accept it and follow it. God has given us three Ps to guide us in seeking a life of true generosity: *percentage, priorities,* and *progress.*

- **Percentage**. God has given us the tithe as a standard for financial giving. In other words, 10 percent of our income is to be set aside to give away. That does not mean that 10 percent is the limit to our giving, just that anything below that level falls short of God's standard. If giving a tithe is new to you, percentage giving is a great place to start —even if you begin with one percent of your income and increase it annually.

- **Priorities**. The illusions of greed and generosity are so well hidden in our lives that we will never overcome them unless we are intentional in the way we handle our finances. Giving has to be a top priority. We do not give as an afterthought or on impulse—in response to a heart-tugging appeal. We have to establish in advance that all of our income is God's, and use that percentage giving toward His priorities.

- **Progress**. I would not expect anyone to go from zero to sixty overnight. Or from 2 percent to 10 percent in a sudden leap forward. If you have not been practicing true generosity and your finances are not yet set up to give away at least 10 percent, you won't be able to make that change in a sudden shift. But you can work your way up to giving 10 percent. You set that as your standard, and you commit to making gradual progress until you achieve it.

Research shows that Americans, and especially American Christ-followers, are some of the most generous people in the world. Yet the average Christ-follower gives away less than 2 percent of his income.

Ronald Sider, author of the book *Rich Christians in an Age of Hunger*, had this to say:

> For Christians in the richest nation in history to be giving only 2.43 percent of their income to their churches is not just stinginess, it is biblical disobedience—blatant sin. We have become so seduced by the pervasive consumerism and materialism of our culture that we hardly notice the ghastly disjunction between our incredible wealth and the agonizing poverty in the world. Over the last 40 years, American Christians (as we have grown progressively richer) have given a smaller and smaller percent of our growing income to the ministries of our churches. Such behavior flatly contradicts what the Bible teaches about God, justice, and wealth. We should be giving not 2.4 percent but 10 percent, 15 percent, even 25 to 35 percent or more to kingdom work. Most of us could give 20 percent and not be close to poverty.[2]

Christianity Today magazine researched the most accurate assessment of what percentage of their income the average American Christ-follower gives away. The magazine reported that the *Chronicle of Philanthropy* noted that donations received by the nation's four hundred biggest charities—religious and otherwise—had dropped by 11 percent. Yet donations received by charities that belong to the Evangelical Council for Financial Accountability remained strong. A report from Empty Tomb, Inc., found that evangelical Christians donate about 4 percent of their income to their churches. Overall, Christians in the United States give 2.43 percent of their income.[3]

Even at the low end of giving at 2.43 percent of income, God has used the financial gifts of American Christ-followers to advance missions, gospel outreaches, hospitals, halfway houses, relief aid, mental hospitals, and schools throughout the world. If that's what God did with less than 3 percent, imagine what would happen if we took seriously God's standard of 10 percent. It's possible to reach that level by progressively working your way up from your current level of giving.

Jesus used a woman who gave all she had as the model of generosity. A widow brought two pennies to the temple and gave them as an offering (see Mark 12:41–44). Because she gave all she had, her generosity affected her livelihood. The gift meant that she would have to live differently as a result.

Godonomics calls for giving not out of what is left over after you have purchased everything you want. Real generosity calls for organizing your life around God's three Ps: percentage, priorities, and progress. If you don't keep God's guidelines constantly in front of you, you will fall victim to the illusion of generosity. That means you will spend and share, but to no one's benefit but your own.

Jesus didn't give to us out of His leftovers; He gave His very best. He left the penthouse for the outhouse. He was born to a poor, working-class family. He knows what it's like to learn a trade, to use tools with skill, to build something with His hands. He left heaven to come to earth, to live among us and teach us, to perform miracles and to live a life that modeled God's will. And then, the sacrifice He gave—His life and His blood—showed us the very best that He could possibly give.

To escape the self-serving lie of the illusion of generosity, study the life of Jesus and set out to follow His example. God doesn't force us to give to others. But He does say, "Look at everything I've given you. I sacrificed My Son for you." When you struggle with true generosity, you don't need to try harder; you need to look deeper into the gift and sacrifice of Jesus Christ.

The sacrifice of Christ is the motivation for you and me to live in a totally new way: devoted to radical generosity and committed to look deeply into our hearts to root out greed.

PART 6

If God Were Talking to Social-Justice Spokesman Jim Wallis

What Would God Say to Jim Wallis About Socialism?

Contrasting biblical justice with the redistribution of wealth

Godonomics is the contemporary application of God's wisdom—and His requirements—for a just, biblical system of economics. This discussion is needed, in part, because our nation's leaders have lost sight of America's founding principles. The discussion is also critical for a second reason: sincere Christians are being influenced by a growing movement that advances socialism as God's favored economic system.

I referred to Jim Wallis in the title of this chapter, not because he is the only high-profile Christian who pushes this agenda, but because he is one of the most outspoken advocates of an erroneous and harmful reinterpretation of "social justice." His approach distorts the meaning of this term, characterizing it as the compassionate and God-honoring corrective to the greed and exploitation that are said to be built into capitalism.

Christians are being lured away from God's wisdom in the realm of economics, and it is time for a clear-eyed look at what Wallis is really saying. Younger Christians, especially, are being won over by persuasive authors, speakers, and bloggers—Wallis and others—who emphasize the priority of helping the poor. They use the term *social justice* to advocate a shift of the economic balance in favor of those who are not producing wealth. These spokesmen do not refer to their preferred economic system as socialism, but their call to ever-increasing government intervention on the part of the government has the same result. Instead, they insist that it is true to Scripture, calling attention to certain practices carried out in ancient Israel. They are reshaping the thinking of Christians in ways that support the shifting of wealth away from those who are the producers in America's economy.

Confusion Among Sincere Christians

I had finished making a presentation on the biblical case for free-market capitalism to about a hundred businessmen in the Cincinnati area. When I opened the floor for questions, the first person asked about the proper role of social justice.

I told the group, "As a follower of Christ, I never use that term. Why? The term has been hijacked by a group that has distanced 'justice' from its historic meaning. Today, 'social justice' is used as a Trojan horse for socialism."

The man responded, "What about charity and generosity? Weren't the early Christians basically communists, sharing with each other as they had need?" He was alluding to this passage in the book of Acts:

> They devoted themselves to the apostles' teaching and to the fellowship, to the breaking of bread and to prayer. Everyone was filled with awe, and many wonders and miraculous signs were done by the apostles. *All the believers were together and had everything in common. Selling their possessions and goods, they gave to anyone as he had need.* (Acts 2:42–45, NIV)

I used some of the question-and-answer time to give needed dimension to this issue.

"The early Christians were committed to generosity," I said, "but that has nothing to do with the modern use of the term *social justice*. Should Christians be generous? Of course! Christianity has been the source of revolutionary generosity. The ethic of Jesus's concern for the poor spread across the Roman Empire from Christianity's beginning. There is no biblical Christian anywhere in the world who would disagree with Jesus's call to His followers as individuals to radically care for the poor and oppressed (see Acts 2:45).

"Further, all the evidence shows that followers of Christ have been the most generous people in history, serving and giving in ways that benefit both religious and nonreligious causes."

I continued. "Although the term *social justice* was first made popular in Roman Catholic theology as a way to challenge individuals to give lavish percentages of their income to help the hurting, in our day the concept is used as a code phrase for 'government interventionism.' And as for your comment regarding the early Christians modeling a communist model for distribution of wealth, Jesus was no more a communist or Marxist than He was a murderer."

The man who had asked the question at first was quiet, but then he followed up. "What do you think God would say about social justice today?"

I paused for a moment before I answered. "Though it's always dangerous to presume to speak for God, I think He would say, 'I do not think *social justice* means what you think it means—at least not anymore.'"

In the movie *The Princess Bride*, a crowd favorite if there ever was one, the characters Inigo Montoya and Vizzini have the following exchange:

MONTOYA: You are sure nobody's following us?
VIZZINI: As I told you, it would be absolutely, totally, and in all other ways inconceivable. No one in Guilder knows what we've done, and no one in Florin could have gotten here so fast. Out of curiosity, why do you ask?

MONTOYA: No reason. It's only... I just happened to look behind us and something is there.

(The next morning, Dread Pirate Roberts is chasing the two men up a mountain.)

VIZZINI: He didn't fall? Inconceivable.
MONTOYA: You keep using that word. I do not think it means what you think it means.[1]

The exchange between the hunted men shows that even seemingly knowledgeable people can misuse words they don't really understand. Nowhere is this truer than in the realm of politics and religion. The phrase *social justice* sounds noble and patriotic. *Social* brings to mind a community, a family, or perhaps even a celebration or a party. *Justice* sounds like standing for what's right and opposing what is wrong. We all like truth, justice, and the American way, so why wouldn't we support social justice?

To gain perspective, let's examine these often-overlooked realities:

- The push for social justice is a Trojan horse that seeks to gain support for socialism in America.
- Jesus was no more a Marxist than He was a murderer.
- Godonomics is based on *real* justice that is the only biblical way to help the poor.

Let's begin by looking at the socialist Trojan horse.

The Socialist Spin on "Social Justice"

Like Vizzini's misuse of the word *inconceivable,* the push for social justice is no longer based on the phrase's original meaning. The term has been hijacked by Marxists who use it to advance their cause by swaying otherwise well-meaning people. That's not to say that all people who use the phrase are socialists. Some are a lot like Vizzini. They talk about social justice thinking that they know what it means, but they have no idea how the term is being subverted and employed in the service of enemies of capitalism. There are even well-meaning, compassionate pastors and church members who don't realize the phrase has been transformed into a falsely Christian imperative.

The prophet Micah instructs followers of God "to do justly, to love mercy, and to walk humbly with your God" (6:8). The word *justice* as used by the prophet is the Hebrew word *mishpat*, which is the action that flows from the humility of having received God's mercy. The same word is used in Leviticus 24:22, where God's people are warned to have the same rule of law (*mishpat*) for foreigners as well as Israelites. God requires the impartial rule of law. Legal disputes must be evaluated based on the merits of the case, not the socioeconomic standing and advantages (or disadvantages) of the plaintiff or the defendant. In fact, *Strong's Lexicon* shows that the word *mishpat*, or "justice," is by far the most common Old Testament word that denotes the impartial rule of law before a judge or a court.[2]

The biblical call to justice is about the rule of law, not the redistribution of assets in society. The Bible never justifies a system in which citizens, through paying taxes, hire the government to steal from one segment of the people (the rich) to give more money, services, and assistance to another segment (the middle class, the working class, and the poor). The Bible never calls us to violate property rights, incentive, or personal liberty through taxation as a way to shift wealth from the top toward the middle and the bottom socioeconomic strata.

The biblical call to the impartial rule of law has proved to be the secret to prosperity and freedom throughout history. When societies enact and enforce laws that make exceptions for one group to the disadvantage of another group, chaos ensues. Further, when governments redefine *justice* to mean "asset redistribution," citizens across the board end up poorer and the regime in power ends up richer.

Economist Milton Friedman explained why the principle of impartial laws undergirds free societies.

> We have learned about the importance of private property and the rule of law as a basis for economic freedom.... Russia privatized but in a way that created private monopolies—private centralized economic controls that replaced government's centralized controls. It turns out that the rule of law is probably more basic than privatization. Privatization is meaningless if you don't have the rule of law. What does it mean to privatize if you do not have security of property, if you can't use your property as you want to?[3]

Those who advocate the modern misuse of the term *social justice* might point to practices described in the Old Testament. Israel did redistribute cash, land, and other assets to the poor, with the help of the priests and the God-prescribed government under Mosaic Law. Such a redistribution had the endorsement of many of the Old Testament prophets, who seemed to consistently side with the cause of the poor against the greed of the powerful and the wealthy. Such Jewish laws and practices as the Year of Jubilee, the forgiveness of debts every seven years, and the law that allowed the hungry and the poor to glean grain from the corners of fields they didn't own are used to advocate in favor of socialist economic policies.

The argument goes like this: God requires such acts to keep the economic playing field more level than it would be if an economy were left unregulated. This same interpretation argues that, by extension, God's followers (in the form of his original chosen nation) lived under a legal code and religious system that required certain practices that shifted wealth from those on the upper rungs down the ladder into the pockets of the needy.

This is not a discussion being carried on only by church members in liberal mainline denominations. Nor is it just a passing fad among a fringe element in the evangelical world. It is a widespread movement among evangelical Christians, and it is now reaching into the mainstream of the evangelical world.

Here is an excerpt from a blog written by a megachurch pastor, making a case for wealth redistribution:

> But this idea of justice being linked to societal systems is all over scripture.
>
> In Israel, even with a king and governance structure in place, they were to hold a major event every fifty years [the Year of Jubilee] where...all debts [were] forgiven...[and] any land that had been bought fair-and-square had to be given back to its original owner, even if the previous owner was a lazy slob, never farmed it and got himself in debt. What's more, all people who were indentured employees because they owed their boss money were set free. Jubilee was a massive social security system—a huge act of social justice and wealth redistribution—that may not seem fair to us free market capitalists but it was vital for Israel.[4]

There are many problems with this interpretation and its application to society today. First, the laws of Israel were parameters that God set up to benefit relationships in a nation of believing people. This was a nation that, until Saul was made king, only had one King, and He was God. And even during the time that Israel was ruled by earthly kings, God still was the nation's recognized Ruler.

Second, ancient Israel was a theocratic nation-state, unlike any nation or political subdivision in existence today. America's founding principles of freedom and justice for all include every citizen, not just those who follow the One True God and adhere to His commands. America's guarantees of liberty and equal legal protections for all citizens stand in stark contrast to radical, extremist nation-states in the Muslim world, where Islamists enforce Sharia law based on the Koran. Sharia law is imposed across the board, without regard to the religious beliefs of individual citizens.

Third, Jesus told us that He has fulfilled (a completed work) the Year of Jubilee. He said, "The Spirit of the LORD is upon Me, because He has anointed Me to preach the gospel to the poor;...to set at liberty those who are oppressed; to proclaim the acceptable year of the LORD.... Today this Scripture is fulfilled in your hearing" (Luke 4:18–19, 21). The Year of Jubilee was about Jesus Christ. It had its fulfillment at the moment when Jesus presented Himself as God's anointed.

Jesus never applied the Old Testament's Year of Jubilee to non-Jewish societal systems. Among His disciples were a government official, Matthew, and an antigovernment zealot, Simon. Both of them would have urged Jesus for a definite statement one way or the other if the Year of Jubilee had still been in effect in the Kingdom of God in the first century.

A Biblical Approach to Relieving Poverty

God's principles lay out a balanced approach to addressing the problem of poverty. While liberals assume poverty is caused by external factors such as class prejudice, limited access to quality education, corporate greed, and the denial of employment opportunities to certain groups, the Bible shows that the causes are more complex. Poverty is caused by a myriad of external and internal factors, including laziness (see Proverbs 6:6–11), lack of a strong work ethic (see Proverbs 12:11), and an absence of self-discipline (see Proverbs 23:21). The Bible also points to external factors that contribute to poverty, such as creditors assessing an oppressive rate of interest (see Exodus 22:25–27), a biased legal system (see Leviticus 19:15), and employers who don't pay employees in a timely manner or according to the Golden Rule (see James 5:1–6).

Despite the Bible's thorough diagnosis of the problem, God has never endorsed Marxist economic theory as a solution to poverty. The redistribution of wealth in a society is not a biblical approach. If we are not careful, we can be misled by the current debate over social justice. It's important to realize that advocates have attached a different meaning to the term and are using it to advance an unbiblical agenda.

In the past, *social justice* referred to an individual's personal generosity directed at helping the poor. St. Thomas Aquinas's use of the phrase made this clear: "Justice is a certain rectitude of mind, whereby a man does what he ought to do in the circumstances confronting him."[5]

However, those who use the term most often today have twisted the meaning, shifting it away from individual responsibility. They use "social justice" to refer to the state or government interfering with a free-market economy in ways that redistribute wealth from the top toward the bottom. In this way, government is called upon to institute and enforce one faction's view of social and economic equality.

Stated another way, *social justice* has been redefined to mean "strict egalitarian distributive justice," defined by *Stanford Encyclopedia of Philosophy* as "strict, or radical, equality. The principle says that every person should have the same level of material goods and services. The principle is most commonly justified on the grounds that people are morally equal and that equality in material goods and services is the best way to give effect to this moral ideal."[6]

Notice the emphasis on radical equality that makes sure everyone has the same level of goods. Of course, that begs the question, Who will take from those who have more and give to those who have less? The answer, of course, is *the government*: "…goods or services are apportioned by an authority (a government agency, for example) on the basis of a commonly accepted standard."[7]

So in the interest of combating poverty, advocates of social justice are quick to call upon the government to violate the rights of the individual by engineering perceived equality among citizens. This sets the stage for an ever-increasing loss of personal liberty. Social justice no longer means what you think it means.

Sometimes a well-meaning person of faith may hang on to a word that has changed meaning in an effort to resist the culture's dictating a new meaning or subverting a word's original definition. When I was attending graduate school, a preaching class I was in was discussing the confusion that is caused when a speaker uses the wrong word at the wrong time.

One man raised his hand. "I gotta share this," he said. "Our pastor has a word he uses every week that does not convey its original meaning."

The teacher said, "Okay, what is it?"

"Each week, our pastor gets up in front of the congregation and says, 'As we come to worship the Lord, I want to hear an ejaculation of praise!'"

This pronouncement was followed by awkward silence and even some snickering from the congregation.) My classmate explained that his pastor knows the word has sexual connotations but insists on holding to its original meaning: "an explosive display of emotion."

This pastor can insist on using the word, but I'm convinced it doesn't mean what he thinks it means. I would guess it has been a turning point for many first-time visitors who never return.

The Trojan Horse Might Be Concealing Liberation Theology

While attending college in 1992 for my undergraduate degrees, I took a class on look-alike theologies. My professor spent a day on liberation theology. This philosophy teaches that Jesus's primary mission on earth was not about forgiveness or atonement (covering of sin), but about freeing the oppressed from the domination of imperialist nations. Theologians from this sector teach that Christ came with a mandate to bless governments and movements that take from the wealthy (who had obviously accrued wealth dishonestly) to give to the poor (who had been exploited by the wealthy). This theology had a large following among Christians in Africa and Latin America.

We studied the record of history, finding that theological teachings consistent with liberation theology eventually led to the rule of enslaving socialism. It promised freedom but opened the way for dictators. One recent example is Hugo Chavez, former president of Venezuela. He regularly spoke of socialism and Jesus in the same breath prior to his death early this year.

"Today is a memorable day," Chavez said after being reelected. "I thank God and ask Him life and health to keep serving the Venezuelan people. I congratulate from my heart the more than eight million Venezuelans who voted for...the revolution, who voted for socialism." He added, "Give me your crown, Jesus. Give me your cross, your thorns so that I may bleed. But give me life, because I have more to do for this country and these people. Do not take me yet."[8]

In addition, Chavez has referred to Jesus as the greatest socialist in history. In 2007, as Venezuela's president was sworn in for his third term in office, he "echoed the famous call to arms of his Cuban mentor. 'Fatherland, socialism or death.'" Then he added, "I swear by Christ, the greatest socialist in history."[9]

Chavez promised to bring more of the benefits of liberation theology to Venezuela. Here are a few highlights from his tenure as president.

> Chávez's 13-year rule has sent Venezuela racing toward the bottom in virtually every indicator that measures economic freedom, rule of law, and ease of doing business. While the Chávez regime reports that economic growth achieved 5.4 percent in the second quarter of 2012, serious economists argue that growth in Venezuela is largely unsustainable and actually decelerating. Economic experts predict severe currency devaluation...and cuts in social spending....

A recent Gallup poll indicates that Venezuela is the country whose residents fear crime the most. The homicide rate is among the highest in the Americas at around 67 per 100,000 inhabitants. For 2011, the Venezuelan Observatory of Violence recorded 19,336 homicides, compared to a reported 4,550 murders in 1998 when Chávez first won election.

Corruption occurs at all levels of government. Former *Foreign Policy* editor Moises Naim warns that interaction between government officials and criminal organizations has created a dangerous "mafia state." Two former senior judges—Eladio Aponte and Luis Velasquez Alvaray—fled Venezuela in 2012 and have provided extensive information to the U.S. regarding the loss of judicial independence, widespread corruption, and drug-trafficking deals among senior officials. Since 2008, the U.S. Treasury Department has designated five serving and former key officials as drug kingpins, including current Defense Minister Henry Rangel Silva.[10]

Don't be deceived by the rhetoric of compassion and fairness that is used by social-justice advocates. Look behind their words to determine if liberation theology influences their thinking. Jim Wallis and his organization, Sojourners, took a stand in favor of a leftist regime in Nicaragua.[11] I fear that Christians who support Wallis's efforts are not checking the facts. He has stated that his magazine received support from globalist-leftist George Soros.[12]

None of this makes Wallis a socialist or a Marxist. But his attempts to characterize himself as an unbiased, moderate voice are disingenuous at best.

If you talk to a Christian—even a pastor—who adheres to the basic principles of liberation theology, you might not immediately discern the difference between that view and true gospel Christianity. The person will most likely quote Jesus and read from Moses and the major prophets. Reverend Jeremiah Wright, President Barack Obama's former pastor in Chicago, is a high-profile example.

I went to college in Chicago, so Wright's name rang a bell when one of his sermons captured headlines in 2008. I checked his church website, which featured a clear statement endorsing the values and emphasis of liberation theology. A few years later, the website statement reflects a minor rewording. The paragraph titled "Mission Statement" now begins, "Trinity United Church of Christ has been called by God to be a congregation that is not ashamed of the gospel of Jesus Christ."[13]

What Christian would disagree with that? Paul, in Romans 1:16, states, "For I am not ashamed of the gospel of Christ, for it is the power of God to salvation for everyone who believes, for the Jew first and also for the Greek."

So far so good, unless two people use different definitions of "the good news," which is what *gospel* means. One of us might mean "I am not ashamed of the message that Christ came to rescue humanity from the power of death by making a way to find forgiveness and spend eternity in heaven when you die." Someone else might mean "I am not ashamed of the message that Christ came to start a political movement focused on speaking against imperialist nations that we deem unjust and to inspire a revolution by those who have been exploited." Those conflicting definitions clarify the true commitments of the speaker.

I continued reading the church's mission statement: "Trinity United Church of Christ has been called by God to be a congregation that is not ashamed of the gospel of Jesus Christ and that does not apologize for its African roots!"[14] When I was pastor of a multiracial church in LaGrange, Georgia, the pastoral team worked tirelessly to value and model racial diversity. Black leaders and white leaders worked together closely in our church. We created worship experiences that crossed racial and economic divides in our area.

As Bible-believing Christians, we believe in one race, the human race. We are all descendants of Adam and are made in the image of God.

The history of Christ-followers has been one of promoting freedom and personal liberty and working against systematic injustice aimed at a particular group or class of people. Christ-followers have been at the forefront of liberating slaves and the oppressed and assisting the hurting.[15] However, standing for what is right and defending those who are unjustly treated is not the same as the gospel. It is rather an implication of the gospel's message wherever it spread.[16]

What is the difference between the gospel and the impact of the gospel? Dr. Luke, an ancient historian, addressed this in a letter he wrote to Theophilus. The letter today is known as the New Testament book of Acts. In the first century, many in Rome were concerned that the new Jesus movement was a political ideology bent on overthrowing the Roman government. Luke went into painstaking detail to show that this was not the case. He wrote that Christianity respected the rule of law, using Paul as an example. Luke tracked Paul's appeal to Caesar and his conversations with Roman leaders, and Luke recorded clear evidence that Roman judges did not feel the growing Jesus movement was a political ideology.

The irony of the gospel is this: by followers of Jesus focusing on individual conversion and the life-on-life experience of God's forgiveness, Rome was turned upside-down. This occurred not through political revolution but through countless personal conversions throughout the empire.

The mission statement of the church formerly pastored by Reverend Wright continues, "Trinity United Church of Christ has been called by God to be a congregation that is not ashamed of the gospel of Jesus Christ and that does not apologize for its African roots! As a congregation of baptized believers, *we are called to be agents of liberation* not only for the oppressed, but for all of God's family" (emphasis added).[17]

I realized the phrase *agents of liberation* was indicative of political liberation theology. This thinking, conveyed in the preaching of Reverend Wright, was also seen in the philosophy of the Obama administration starting in 2009. While the president publicly repudiated Wright's sermon in which the pastor repeated "God d--n America" and Obama distanced himself from

Wright's rhetoric in general, the principles of liberation theology are evident in Obama's policies. (And don't forget that Jim Wallis serves as one of the president's advisors.)

Further, President Obama was exposed to liberation theology at Wright's church for more than twenty years. And as we have seen, liberation theology insinuates itself into a person's thinking through the Trojan horse of such righteous-sounding terms as *social justice.*

This is not at all consistent with the work of Dr. Martin Luther King Jr. and other leaders of the civil rights movement. King quoted the Declaration of Independence's phrase "all men are created equal," noting that our nation's founders showed that the law of nature gave government only a few limited roles. The primary one was to protect the individual liberties that we are endowed with by our Creator. He did *not* argue that the government was commissioned to redistribute wealth. A legal guarantee of rights for all people was rightly seen as the legitimate application of the impartial rule of law. King, a Republican, led people in speaking against the evils of injustice without trying to change the gospel message.

I met another strong, nonviolent civil rights leader when I lived in La-Grange, Georgia. My dentist, a thirty-year-old black woman, told me about her years in junior high school standing with her father against the evils of racial segregation. Even in the 1980s, the community she lived in maintained separate schools for black students. She shared the terror she felt standing in the city square as the Ku Klux Klan marched through the downtown area. Her father squeezed her hand as Klan members screamed at them, called them names, and spat on this innocent little girl and her dad. My heart broke as I pictured the hatred she had to endure. She told me that her father would lean over and whisper, "They're wrong, but remember Jesus loves them too."

She shared how this powerful combination of truth and grace shaped her character. Her father was her hero as he stood against the bigotry of the Klan while refusing to advocate hatred or a violent response.

Courageous people of faith stand for what is right and oppose evil. The call for government to protect individuals' God-given rights is consistent with the government's proper role. Justice is about equal access to the rule of law, in contrast to social justice, which advocates using the government to take from one group in order to give to another. That is an important distinction, and it shows why we need to use discernment. Words and phrases can act as Trojan horses. The *gospel* still means "the good news of salvation" to most Christians, but a growing movement is redefining the word to mean "social and political revolution." As a result, gospel Christianity can easily be confused with liberation theology if you are not looking to see what is inside the Trojan horse.

What Would God Say to Jim Wallis About the Rule of Law?

Jesus did not recruit revolutionaries to overthrow an earthly empire

S ocial justice has become the battle cry of a new generation of church leaders. This emphasis has helped point members of generation Y and the millennial generation toward community service and helping the poor. At the same time, however, social-justice advocates have smuggled in Marxist theory. At their most candid, some leaders in this movement portray Jesus as a Marxist figure whose reason for coming to earth was to help the little people.[1]

I attribute much of this thinking, writing, and speaking to a naive understanding of the dangers, brutality, and inhumanity of communism. Yet in spite of the lengthy and bloody historical record of Marxism's exploitation and abuses, I continue to hear Christians—including many in pastoral and other leadership roles—portray Jesus in a way that would enshrine Him in a North Korean Hall of Heroes.

It is time to counter this false teaching with clear-eyed facts. Marx and Jesus saw the world totally differently. Marx was an atheist who saw "God" as a projection of man's radical alienation from his psyche and his labor, due to the oppression of the bourgeois. In stark contrast, Jesus saw God as the ultimate Source of meaning and purpose and as the very definition of truth, all of which lead us to love God and others. Jesus taught that work and labor were gifts from God. Jesus befriended the rich and poor alike while affirming that all people need God's grace to transform them from the inside out.

Marx thought religion was a psychological problem that created internal unrest. He taught that salvation lay not in heaven coming to earth but with humanity creating heaven on earth. He concurred with others who had given up on what they believed to be the delusion of God and heaven, believing that they could build a utopia by having the right people in power.

Impatient Marxist leader Vladimir Lenin taught that a revolutionary catalyst should be applied to speed up the creation of a utopian society. Lenin's oppression of the poor led to starvation and widespread death in the Soviet Union. A small group of "redistributors" took the lion's share of the nation's resources while they doled out crumbs to the little people.

Further, Lenin hated Christianity and recognized the message of the Bible as the most powerful challenger to his ideology. Neither Lenin nor Marx considered Jesus to be a Marxist, so why would any of Jesus's followers accept that portrayal of Him? The Marxist goal of the redistribution of wealth through force is not a biblical teaching. Instead, Scripture emphasizes humanity's inability to produce a perfect society as well as our helplessness when it comes to rescuing ourselves from eternal destruction.

The gospel teaches that each individual is in need of a Rescuer who offers forgiveness and right standing with God. The gospel teaches that God came to earth and made a way to rescue all who would turn from their waywardness. The implications of God's sacrificial love are astounding! The God of the universe searched for us when we were lost. God came to us when we were poor and indebted to Him spiritually, offering to credit our spiritual account with vast heavenly treasures!

When we respond to that kind of God-love, we are compelled to go out looking for the poor and the forgotten to pay forward the grace we've received. This is what the Bible teaches, not a Marxist social-justice look-alike. The gospel has nothing to do with state-sponsored redistribution of wealth. It is not about calling on government to take what one person produces to give to another person.

Marxism Blocks the Real Solutions to Poverty

Marxists not only misdiagnose social and economic problems, but they compound the problem by offering a failed system as the solution. Governmental intervention—or *statism*—creates problems that have the effect of blocking the promised solution. This could be the definition of irony. And to compound the problem, Marxism increases the people's demand for the failed solutions of governmental intervention. Social-justice Christians misdiagnose the problem by assuming that capitalism is bad. Then they compound the problem by insisting that more governmental intervention is the solution. In the process they turn sincere people of faith into willing co-conspirators of the government. They convince people that the most beneficial social and economic policy requires citizens to hand over their prosperity, liberty, and productivity to the most unresponsive, corrupt, and inefficient institutional system: government. This shows how socialism serves as a steppingstone to Marxism. It is the gradual destruction of individual liberty and private-property rights.

Socialism, Marxism, and communism share three guiding principles in common: to nationalize the private sector, to suppress the free market, and to increase government control. And though there are shades of difference between the three, the outcome is the same. They demonize the proven solution of free-market capitalism and seek to replace it with the failed system of centralized governmental control.

Advocates of social justice are, in fact, advancing the cause of corrupt and coercive forms of government. The government's takeover of the private sector operates under many different names, but it always seeks to nationalize business, commerce, and private property. This pattern has played out since ancient times, from the pharaohs of ancient Egypt to the expansion and exploitation of Imperial Rome. It has continued throughout history, resurfacing in virulent forms during the twentieth century with Hitler's Nazi Germany, Stalin's Soviet Union, and Hugo Chavez's takeover of private industry in Venezuela.

A careful study of history shows that free-market capitalism offers the proven solution to poverty. Capitalism's principles of work, incentive, and job creation are the engines that empower the poor. Capitalism frees up individuals to share their profits in ways that assist and empower the poor. Free enterprise offers the poor what they need most: employment opportunities that enable them to use their talents to become self-reliant.

In stark contrast, government powerbrokers espouse the *idea* that all people are equal while hypocritically operating on the basis that some people (meaning the powerbrokers) are *more* equal than others. Rather than passing laws that are impartial examples of biblical justice applying to all people equally, they make exceptions for themselves and their friends, primary among them campaign donors and others who can do them favors. You will not hear the powerbrokers of either major political party tell the truth about the superiority of real, free-market capitalism, because doing so would limit their power and their need to be needed.

Marxism Is Social *In*justice

The Reverend Al Sharpton is a leading voice for social justice. He is known to have said, "The dream was not to put one black family in the White House. The dream was to make everything equal in everybody's house."[2]

Sharpton's statement has more in common with the Communist Manifesto than the Holy Scriptures. Marxism promises asset equality, while Jesus's parable of the talents does not.

The website Social Justice Definition defines *social justice* in connection with the distribution of assets in society: "Social justice is equivalent to social fairness. It is a phrase that refers to giving what is rightly due to an individual or group, team or community.... Social justice is about equality and fairness between human beings."[3]

Clearly, this is not a definition that a discerning Christ-follower could endorse as being consistent with the Bible's teachings. Yet many Christians advocate government-mandated social engineering by quoting passages from the Bible about justice for the downtrodden and helping widows and orphans. The use of such "justice passages" to support governmental intervention in wealth distribution is faulty hermeneutics.

Jim Wallis, in a blog post titled "How Christian Is Tea Party Libertarianism?" wrote,

> Just look at the biblical prophets in their condemnation of injustice to the poor, and how they frequently follow those statements by requiring the king (the government) to act justly (these requirements applied both to the kings of Israel and to foreign potentates). Jeremiah, speaking of King Josiah, said, "He defended the cause of the poor and needy, and so all went well" (Jeremiah 22:16). Amos instructs the courts (the government) to "Hate evil, love good; maintain justice in the courts" (Amos 5:15). The prophets hold kings, rulers, judges, and employers accountable to the demands of justice and mercy.[4]

Wallis is correct in saying that the Bible stresses the need for government to be involved in justice (discerning right and wrong, meting out punishment to wrongdoers) and making sure people receive impartial treatment under the law—regardless of economic or social status. The government has a responsibility to punish evil and enforce the rule of law, or *mishpat*. A government's job (biblically, as well as in libertarian governmental theory) is to protect the rights of the individual, enforce contracts, and substantiate the rule of law. When a government begins to treat people differently based on their economic status, Christ-followers should stand up and speak against the tyranny. Wallis cites this reality in his quotation of Amos 5:15, where Amos addressed the "courts" (NIV) about the need for justice, that being equal enforcement of law.

When King Ahab (the government) tried to violate the property rights of Naboth (an individual), the prophet Elijah spoke up. Ahab wanted to take possession of Naboth's vineyard, but Naboth didn't want to sell. Rather than protecting the property rights of this individual, Ahab and his wife, Jezebel, had Naboth killed. This was not only murder but an example of governmental exploitation. It was the responsibility of the people and the prophets to speak up against it (see 1 Kings 21).

Wallis was correct in saying the Bible defines a role for government in keeping justice, meaning enforcing the rule of law; providing for national defense; enforcing contracts; and punishing evil. In light of these legitimate roles of government, a limited taxation of citizens is justified.

But he missed the boat in his Tea Party critique when he cited God's view of kings. God had warned the people in 1 Samuel 8 that asking for a king was a bad idea. Samuel warned the people that kings would not impartially enforce justice (the rule of law) but would instead steal from the people, violate their property rights, and impose burdensome taxation. So whenever a passage in the Bible speaks to a king, God is speaking about a system that is not in His Plan A.

God set up laws to govern His people. The list of hundreds of moral concepts can be summarized in the Ten Commandments, which outline the ways to best preserve a free society. Among this top-ten summary is "Thou shalt not covet" (Exodus 20:17, KJV). Social-justice advocates who insist on governmental intervention to bring about the redistribution of wealth are endorsing two acts that God explicitly condemns. No government is justified in intervening to supply to one group what it covets (the poor coveting the wealth of the producers) by stealing from the producers through taxation to hand wealth to the poor.

Christ-followers have a personal responsibility to share with, give to, and help those who are hurting. The battle cry for charity should be loud and long to the entire society, calling every citizen to give in ways that help those in need. This is a far cry from leveraging the power of government to steal from some in order to give to others.

John Adams, the second president of the United States, said, "'Thou shalt not covet' and 'Thou shalt not steal'...must be made inviolable precepts in every society before it can be civilized or made free."[5]

The Bible doesn't support anarchy but instead lays out specific roles a government should and should not perform. It is important to note that the Bible lays out limits to government but not the elimination of government altogether. Understanding this point is helpful in further evaluating Wallis's critique of limited government and his advocacy for social justice.

Wallis has written, "An anti-government ideology just isn't biblical. In Romans 13, the apostle Paul...describes the role and vocation of government; in addition to the church, government also plays a role in God's plan and purposes. Preserving the social order, punishing evil and rewarding good, and protecting the common good are all prescribed; we are even instructed to pay taxes for those purposes!"[6]

There are two problems with those assertions. First, Wallis presumes that the Tea Party is advocating for anarchy rather than limited government. Wallis creates a straw-man argument by claiming that Tea Partiers are suggesting the Bible says there is absolutely no role for government. I don't know of anyone (except anarchists) who would hold such an unreasonable perspective. The second problem with Wallis's statements is his use of the phrase "protecting the common good." This is the Trojan horse that smuggles socialism into the debate. The common good as described in Paul's letter to the Romans is the need for consistent, fair, impartial rule of law. If Wallis were pointing out the evil of government having one healthcare law that applies to members of Congress while a different law applies to the general public, that would be a good application of the biblical call for justice.

Ironically, by endorsing the rule of law, Wallis is advocating for the pillars of economic freedom, because free-market capitalism cannot survive without the rule of law. The Cato Institute (a libertarian research think tank) supports this view, stating that countries that uphold the rule of law offer more economic opportunity for the poor than is provided in socialist, Marxist, or communist countries. The Cato Institute states,

> Freedom of exchange and market coordination provide the fuel for economic progress. Without exchange and entrepreneurial activity coordinated through markets, modern living standards would be impossible.
>
> Potentially advantageous exchanges do not always occur. Their realization is dependent on the presence of sound money, rule of law, and security of property rights, among other factors.[7]

It is interesting to note that in Wallis's blog post he is arguing from the Bible to support the principles of the Libertarians that he is trying to critique. He affirms the Bible's insistence on the rule of law, which is an underpinning of economic freedom. This could be an oversight on his part or a lack of understanding of economic theory. The results are the same. In his blog post, Wallis confirms that the Bible supports free-market capitalism and the limited role of government.[8]

I know a defense lawyer in Atlanta who, for the most part, represents Spanish-speaking immigrants. He noticed a consistent pattern, in which his Spanish-speaking clients were left in jail without access to their phone calls or attorney consultation several days longer than his English-speaking clients. Spanish-speaking clients were treated differently—and badly—by court personnel. The attorney asked me what he should do. If he went before the judge to mention these patterns, it could get him on the bad side of the judge, negatively affecting his newly formed practice. However, what he was observing was not fair, moral, or an impartial application of the law.

I challenged him to stand up for *true* social justice. I suggested he respectfully speak to the judge about the injustice and lack of respect shown for the individual liberty of his Spanish-speaking clients. He followed through by using his power and influence to speak on behalf of the powerless. He appealed to the government to do what's right. That's the true application of biblical social justice.

My friend's boldness in speaking for the less powerful changed the environment and made the judge and jailers aware of some of the unintentional—as well as the intentional—double standards that were being applied.

Godonomics Promotes Real Justice to Help the Poor

Jesus made it clear that the poor would always be with us (see Matthew 26:11). But God has a plan. He wants individuals—not the government—to identify the poor and get help to them. Many of our Founding Fathers understood that caring for the poor is not a legitimate role of government. George Washington and Thomas Jefferson (author of the Declaration of Independence) served on the vestry boards of their churches. They knew that charity is best implemented by private institutions. In their roles as private citizens, they presented needs to church members in keeping with the challenge from Isaiah: "Is this not the fast that I have chosen?... Is it not to share your bread with the hungry, and that you bring to your house the poor who are cast out; when you see the naked, that you cover him, and not hide yourself from your own flesh?" (Isaiah 58:6–7).

The new social-justice version of that verse would swap out a few words of verse 7. It would read something like this: "Is it not to share *the government's* bread with the hungry, and that *the government* brings to *someone else's* house the poor who are cast out; when *the government* sees the naked, that *the government* cover him, and not hide from *the government the government's* own resources?"

Private charity is powerful. Limiting taxes and restricting government control and intrusion would make it even more effective and extensive. The National Institute on Philanthropy monitors every major charitable group in the United States. The institute reports the amount, measured by percentage, of a contribution that ends up going to the recipient. If you donate a dollar to Charity X and sixty cents (60 percent) makes it to the people being helped, Charity Watch would give Charity X a grade of C, because it used a relatively high 40 percent of its donations to cover overhead and other organizational expenses. Higher grades go to charities that operate on a lower percentage of the funds that are donated.

Any guess what percentage of revenue is used by the government to cover overhead? Since 1950, the federal government has taken nine trillion dollars from citizens to help the poor. Yet only *30 percent* made it to those who received the government's help.

The Cato Institute tracks and reports on instances of wasteful spending by the federal government.

> The Coburn report finds that taxpayers have been paying for every-
> thing from robotic squirrels to talking urinal cakes. Did you know
> that people in their 30s who consume lots of alcohol feel immature?
> Thanks to a study funded by the National Institutes of Health, now
> you do. Feeling down but don't want to get drunk because then you'll
> feel immature? Another study funded by the NIH found that you'll
> feel more chipper if you simply turn on the television and watch
> re-runs....
>
> Take the numerous examples in the Coburn report of federal
> money being wasted on subsidies to state and local government.
> Every year the Department of Transportation gives Oklahoma

$150,000 for an airport that receives one flight a month. Beverly Hills, California received $180,000 from a HUD program that's supposed to help spur economic development in lower-income locales. The Department of Commerce and the USDA teamed up to provide over $1 million to help a county in New York build a new yogurt factory for PepsiCo, Inc.[9]

God's plan, outlined in the principles of Godonomics, is much more efficient. Individuals see the needs of the poor and provide help directly. Individualized charity is positioned to better assess real need and to do a better job of determining who is cheating the system. Smaller organizations are more personal. Churches and parachurch groups have more accountability to donors and the ability to quickly customize their approaches to fit current needs. Meanwhile, the government continues to look at ways to penalize citizens for helping the poor. The federal government has considered discontinuing the income-tax deduction allowed for charitable giving. While we should give whether we get a tax break or not, why would a government want to de-incentivize the most efficient method available to help those who need our assistance?[10]

God's concern for the poor is a theme throughout Scripture. His strongest words are reserved for those who have much yet ignore those who have little. Even the famous destruction of Sodom and Gomorrah was primarily about a lack of concern for the powerless and poor (see Ezekiel 16:49–50).

Still, social-justice advocates assume that those who support a free market and point to the Bible's opposition to government intrusion are also opposed to helping the poor. Here are the facts: Christians who advocate conservative, free-market principles are practicing the most effective approaches to overcoming poverty. Free-market advocates emphasize a strong work ethic, incentive, private-sector job creation, and radical personal generosity. Christ-followers who critique the modern social-justice movement are not ignorant of history's recipe for rescuing the poor. By advancing free enterprise, they argue, more jobs will be created, more charity will be extended, and more prosperity will be available for everyone.

At the same time, Christ-followers also need to ask, "If the government were to stop helping the poor, would the church and the private sector *really* step up?" Christ-followers have to think through how their core convictions play out in everyday life. What does it take, on a practical level, to provide help to those who need it?

We live in a broken world where God's ideal will rarely be upheld. We should ask ourselves how we can be on a trajectory toward His ideals. America has been on a trajectory away from God's principles of liberty, productivity, and generosity for a very long time. The free-enterprise system, while still functioning better here than in other regions of the world, is slowly being overtaken by government interventionism. Christ-followers should move to turn the tide. We should hear the record of history warning us about the perils of continuing on this trajectory.

America will probably never return to the constitutional principles set up by our nation's founders, which did not establish a nation that relied on borrowing, inflating the currency, and mortgaging our future. But just because we will never have the ideal doesn't mean we must accept a prolonging of the financial ordeal we are in. We need to come together as Americans and people of faith and commit to moving our country back on a trajectory toward God.

We need to launch an open, productive dialogue and stop demonizing those who disagree with us. We need to ask hard questions and seek workable, nonpartisan answers. If we allow government to take away personal liberties instead of protecting them, doesn't that lead to a gradual, complete loss of freedom? If government programs are far more wasteful than private enterprise, shouldn't we get on a trajectory toward growing business and shrinking government? Does a society of dependence on others really set people up for success?

And we can't avoid asking the hard questions of ourselves and of the faith community. If churches are not acting to help the poor, wouldn't God rather have the government do it than to have people go hungry and without shelter? It is convicting to ask ourselves, "If everyone gave to the poor and hurting at the level of my giving, what kind of society would we have?

Christ-followers must allow God's words to challenge our ideologies. We must never compromise God's truth and blueprint for freedom, but we need to change the methods we use to explain that blueprint to a variety of audiences. In a world that pushes opponents to hate one another, we need to be beacons of tolerance and love to those who hold views that conflict with ours.

Christ-followers should recognize that greed is a serious problem for government and for business both. Neither sector of our nation is immune to exploitation of the weak. Christ-followers must acknowledge that government has a role to play in punishing evil without becoming the evil it is called to repress. We must passionately argue for the poor, the orphan, and the alien to be heard while acknowledging the rule of law and the inefficiencies of public programs.

Christ-followers must let go of political rhetoric and bumper-sticker slogans. We must anchor our principles and motivations in God's text, not *Atlas Shrugged* or the doctrines of MoveOn.org. We must call people to bring *shalom*—peace—to the chaos of our world. We must lead the way in championing the kingdom of God.

Be careful if you are attracted to the social-justice cause. Be equally careful if you have been influenced by a purely utilitarian approach to balancing the federal budget and leaving those who need help to fend for themselves. Rather than following the leading trends, be wise and discerning. Become a student of truly biblical social justice so you can be an effective, results-oriented advocate for freedom as well as for the needy.

PART 7

If God Were
Talking to Karl Marx

What Would God Say to Karl Marx About America?

The United States is unmatched in creating economic prosperity

K arl Marx claimed to have developed an economic system that offered more freedom to the common people. But when his philosophy was put into practice, socialist economics opened the door for a ruling elite to control, and profit from, even more of the common people's livelihood.

Marxism stands in sharp contrast to Godonomics. God wants us to experience liberty, prosperity, and generosity. Marx's view of economics grew out of his atheistic philosophy, which will later overlap with Ivan Pavlov's psychology. He believed individuals' behaviors are programmed by their environment and that human behavior could be taught through specific, selective stimuli. Believing that humanity is inherently good, he taught that all social ills must be the result of the effects of the environment. He set out to fix the problems of society by attempting to manufacture a utopia. He believed this would be accomplished by granting power to the state.

Here is an accurate summary of Marxist economic theory:

Economics is central to Marxism-Leninism because Marx believed that the economic system of a society determines the nature of all legal, social and political institutions. Because the Marxist believes that modes of production form the foundation for society, he concludes that anything wrong with society is the result of imperfect modes of production. Societies have been improving because the economic systems on which they have been founded are gradually improving: slavery gave way to feudalism, and feudalism to capitalism. Because of flaws in capitalism, it will give way to socialism. In a socialist society, all private property will gradually be abolished and man will no longer oppress his fellow man in an effort to protect his private property. When all private property and consequently all class distinctions have withered away, the slow transition from socialism to the highest economic form, communism, will be complete. The ultimate aim of Marxism-Leninism is the creation of a political world order based on communism that will solve the economic problem of scarcity so efficiently that each individual will see his every need, and most of his wants, fulfilled.[1]

Marx's hatred of capitalism and business owners was a pillar of his worldview. America was founded on a totally different view of life, liberty, and the pursuit of happiness, as stated in the Declaration of Independence.

The Proven Record of the United States

It is helpful to talk in real-world terms rather than economic theory. What has capitalism produced in the way of a nation's strength, security, and stability and the prosperity and liberty of its people? To answer that, let's look at the great experiment of the United States.

America was built on a worldview that is 180 degrees opposite of that of Karl Marx and socialism. Our nation's founders relied on a reference point that is based on the role of God and people in government. They put into practice biblical principles that resulted, eventually, in liberty for an entire society. More than two hundred years later, what are the results? America is the world's greatest example on a national level of liberty, prosperity, and generosity.

If you landed on planet Earth and discovered that 4 percent of the world's population created and produced the most playwrights, the most inventions, the most ideas, and the most economic prosperity in history, you would ask, "What's different about that 4 percent?" As you look at the factors that inspired the founders of most hospitals, shelters, private schools, orphanages, and other charitable organizations, you see that their generous spirit can be traced to the liberty, prosperity, and generosity of the American spirit and the values and priorities of people of faith.

Every February, fifty to eighty doctors, nurses, and home builders from our church go to Belize to help the poor, heal the sick, and build homes in the village of San Padro. The poverty level there is heartbreaking, but the spirit of the people is inspiring. Families live in shacks that are only partially walled, built out of cardboard and cast-off linoleum floor covering. Their homes offer only minimal protection from the elements and no protection from mosquitoes.

One of our teams brought rolls of screening to staple over window openings to keep out disease-carrying insects. As our team went door to door, it was often hard to find enough wood in a house's framing to use in securing the screen. Our work on their homes gave us opportunities to invite families to the free medical clinic that our nurses and pharmacists had set up.

During seven days, our team of surgeons and other medical professionals offered free surgeries to anyone who came to the hospital. One team rebuilt an ear for a girl who had been injured in a fire. Another team built two homes from the ground up for a young man with cerebral palsy. In his early years, he had crawled from hut to hut for survival. A villager taught him to walk, and the village rallied around him. Now in his twenties with no real resources, he was ecstatic to see American Christians building his first home.

People received free medicines and pharmaceutical supplies. Families walked through the front doors of their own homes for the first time.

Why such an outpouring of generosity from a team of volunteers? At the commissioning service for one of the new homes, a team member stood before the villagers. He said, "These gifts are not only gifts from the people of the United States but also a gift from Christ. We are not representatives of America; we are representatives of Christ and His gift to us. Jesus taught us that whenever we heal, help, or provide for anyone, it's as if we have been giving to God Himself. We thank you for letting us serve you and serve Christ."

The Telling Contrasts Between Capitalism and Marxism

My analysis of Marxism, and the stark contrasts between a statist economy and capitalism, are influenced by the thinking and research of Ohio Congressman Bob McEwen. He is a personal friend, and his speeches and views on these issues have changed my thinking about the ripple impact of American liberty.[2]

The United States is so prosperous that even our poor are rich compared to people in most of the world. Fifty percent of the world's population lives on two dollars a day or less. Half of that 50 percent lives on less than one dollar a day. The poor in America usually have air conditioning, a car, a television, and a telephone.

The comparative prosperity of all Americans can be linked directly to the productivity and wealth produced in a free-market economy. Consider the following examples contrasting some of America's states with the wealth of foreign nations.

Russia, even with all its gold, oil reserves, and other natural resources, has a gross domestic product (GDP) that falls behind that of California. Russia's GDP ranks slightly ahead of Texas and the state of New York. And when you consider the combined GDP of the twenty-six Arab nations, with all of their petroleum resources, you get a total GDP that is less than half the GDP of California.

Why do individual states in the United States produce more wealth than entire nations or, in the case of the Arab world, twenty-six nations combined? It comes down to one thing: liberty. The freedom enjoyed by individual Americans and American business and industry produces an unmatched level of prosperity.

The Bible establishes a clear link between liberty and the well-being of the people. "And you shall consecrate the fiftieth year, and proclaim liberty throughout all the land to all its inhabitants" (Leviticus 25:10). This verse is inscribed on the Liberty Bell, which commemorates the fiftieth anniversary of William Penn's Charter of Privileges that formed Pennsylvania's first constitution. When God led Israel out of the bondage of Egypt, He taught them how to be a free people. His Law outlined the principles of God-given "inalienable rights" for all people. It taught the bedrock concepts of property rights and the rule of law, which maximize freedom and prosperity. Even our nation's religious freedom finds its basis in the Christian theology of free will. Throughout the Bible, God lays out the path to freedom, but He never forces His people to walk in it. Penn knew that coercion was foreign to the God of the Bible, and that it would never result in economic prosperity.

"Now the Lord is the Spirit; and where the Spirit of the Lord is, there is liberty" (2 Corinthians 3:17). The Liberty Bell's words from Leviticus remind us to not keep a good thing to ourselves. God commissioned the nation of Israel to "proclaim freedom to *all* the inhabitants of the land" (Leviticus 25:10, GNT). The message of God cannot be separated from the message of liberty.

Throughout history, internal liberty has led to external liberty. Men and women of faith fought for the elimination of infanticide in the Roman Empire. Godly leaders, both black and white, marched together in the civil rights movement in America. In Africa and India today, women are learning from followers of Christ that they are made in God's image, are co-heirs with Christ, and are granted special talents and gifts from the God of the universe. Recently I read an article tracking the impact of Christ's teaching in African countries. This journalist called Christianity the greatest revolution for women's rights in Africa.

Freedom costs too much to keep it to ourselves. If the economic domino effect begins with an initial domino of freedom, then we must spread freedom. For wherever there is freedom, there is prosperity. Wherever there is prosperity, there can be incredible generosity. Let's look at all three aspects of the first domino of liberty: the scale, the purchase, and the worldview. We will look at the purchase and worldview in the next chapter. For now, let's take a close look at the scale.

The First Aspect of Liberty: The Scale

Imagine that a scale, ranging from zero to one hundred, represents your paycheck. This is a taxation scale, and the range goes from slavery (zero) to freedom (one hundred). The scale represents the percentage of money and profit that the producer (you) is allowed to keep.

If you are able to keep all of your income, you of course enjoy much more freedom. But if you are left with none of your income, you are enslaved. A

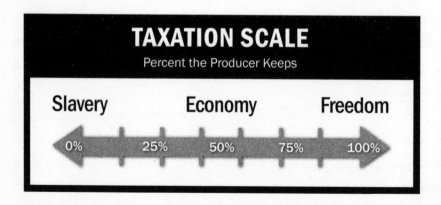

person who keeps 100 percent of her income has more choices. The more money you retain, the more options are open to you. In contrast, when a portion of your income is not available to you, due to taxes, fees, indebtedness, or other salary reductions, you always lose a measure of freedom.

The more income we lose through taxes and other reductions, the fewer choices are open to us and the more our standard of living declines. If someone told you they intended to take half your income, you would start looking for ways to prevent it from happening. How could you agree to lose half your standard of living because of a decision made by an outside party?

The essence of freedom is having choices. In developed nations, especially,

TAXATION IN FOUR NATIONS

	Income Tax	Corporate Tax	Indirect
Sweden	57.77%	26.3%	25% VAT
Canada	50.00%	34.0%	5–15% GST, HST, PST
Denmark	51.50%	25.0%	25% sales and VAT
USA	35.00%	35.0%	0%

Source: www.taxrates.cc (November 2010). Politicians in other countries come up with acronyms for taxation like VAT (value added tax), GST (goods and services tax), HST (harmonized sales tax), and PST (provincial sales tax). Regardless of the terminology, less of your money makes it into your paycheck.

COMPARING TAX RATES

Two-parent household @ $65,000 per year	Local and federal taxes
Sweden	51.5 %
Canada	29.6 %
United States	26.5 %

Source: www.taxrates.cc

citizens are accustomed to paying taxes. A group known as TaxRates.cc compares individual, corporate, and indirect tax rates around the globe. The average tax rate globally, reported for 2010, was 24.99 percent for corporations, 29.40 percent for individuals, and 15.61 percent for indirect taxes. If you look at America today compared to more socialistic or interventionist societies, our total rate of taxation (including corporate, personal, and indirect taxes) is relatively low in comparison. Americans are free to hold on to more of their wealth and, as a result, have more choices. Economic freedom—the liberty to pursue economic opportunities—is critical to political freedom.

Every leader takes us in one direction or the other on the scale from freedom to slavery. Are we moving toward more freedom and individual prosperity, or is a leader moving us toward reduced wealth and, eventually, slavery? To help assess what direction the scale is moving, here are two principles that hold true:

- The greater the freedom, the greater the wealth.
- The greater the government, the greater the poverty.

When a government claims 30 percent or more of your income and redirects it through government bureaucracy, poverty follows. The United States has gradually been moving away from free-enterprise principles since its founding. Socialistic policies have gained ground, including the progressive income tax, fiat currencies (rather than a monetary system that is backed by actual assets), and escalating government intervention that exceeds what is allowed in the Constitution.

A consuming government will attempt to justify its financial coercion by saying, "We're providing lots of beneficial services for that price." But what would happen if as much as 50 percent of personal wealth in a nation were confiscated and redirected through the most inefficient and, often, the most corrupt organizational structure in that country? It would very quickly lead to widespread poverty.

Centralized management of wealth is guaranteed to be wasteful and is destined to fail. Why? The individual knows best how to invest his or her money. The more money individuals bring home, the greater their freedom, their range of choices, and their prosperity. This produces wealth not only for individuals and families, but also for the nation as a whole.

The legitimate role of government is to referee the game, not compete in it. The government is responsible to protect citizens from fraud, to ensure the enactment of free-exchange contracts, and to guard individual citizens from coercion. Thomas Jefferson made this statement:

> A wise and frugal government, which shall restrain men from injuring one another, shall leave them otherwise free to regulate their own pursuits of industry and improvement, and shall not take from the mouth of labor the bread it has earned. This is the sum of good government.[3]

Our nation's founders were careful to specify that the government's role in protecting individuals was as an impartial referee. But the system is turned upside-down when the referees start playing the game. The game comes apart when the government starts committing fraud and coercing the citizens, rather than protecting them from fraud and force.

The following continuum shows the downward spiral into poverty that comes when economic freedom is chipped away. Any political subdivision, from local to state to national, can be placed on this continuum.

TAXATION SCALE
Percent the Producer Keeps

Slavery	Economy	Freedom
0% 25% 50% 75% 100%		

Once you see where a city, for instance, lands on the scale, you can map its trajectory. Take a large city such as Detroit, Michigan. Detroit was once a wealthy city. In 1950, Detroit was number one on the list of the wealthiest large cities in America. But then, greedy leaders and politicians began taking the city down the path of poverty. They increased the level of taxation and regulation. They sucked economic freedom away from individuals and companies.[4]

Today, of the twenty-six largest cities in America, Detroit is the second poorest. The downward spiral of poverty picked up steam as the city moved down the scale, taking more and more from the private sector and funneling more and more to the government's public sector. The city government took away the ability of local businesses to make the best decisions for growth and profitability. Instead, business was straitjacketed by rising taxes, increased regulation, and a variety of payroll restrictions. William McGurn, a *Wall Street Journal* columnist, described the economic spiral that has hurt the entire state of Michigan:

> Michigan today is not a struggling state like California or New Jersey
> or even Wisconsin. It is a basket case, with worse to come if things
> do not change quickly—especially in the relation of the public to
> the private sector. "Many of the protesters seem to think the war is
> between rich and poor," says Michael LaFaive, director of the Morey
> Fiscal Policy Initiative at the Michigan-based Mackinac Center. "But
> the real class war today is between government and the people who
> pay for it. And the government's been winning."[5]

The promised benefits and protections of government regulation and higher taxation never come about. Instead, individuals and businesses lose wealth and freedom without gaining any additional advantages.

Michael Barone of the *Washington Examiner* wrote, "When people ask me why I moved from being a liberal to being a conservative, my single-word answer is Detroit. The liberal policies which I hoped would make Detroit something like heaven have made it instead something more like hell."[6]

The last time my family was in Detroit, we visited the Henry Ford Museum. We were amazed at the role Detroit played in the development and advancement of transportation. Ford's company began to produce, profit, save, and invest in future jobs, and millions were blessed because of it. Detroit was turned into a blueprint for economic growth—until the government started limiting the freedom of business to create wealth.

No city, state, or nation is ever static on the taxation scale. We always are moving in one direction or the other. Marx promised great programs and economic liberty. What the "little people" didn't see is that he offered a service with one hand and took away liberty and prosperity with the other.

Perhaps your father or grandfather fought in the Korean War. The Korean Peninsula is divided into two nations. South Korea enjoys the benefits of liberty; North Korea is the world's leading example of centralized control. The two countries have the same type of people, same language, and same ethnic culture. When the land was divided, North Korea got the better land with less mountainous terrain. The land of the north was easier to cultivate, holding the potential for greater production of food and the greater prosperity. South Korea had to contend with an influx of refugees and more mountainous land, both of them working against the best prospects for economic prosperity. However, South Koreans got freedom, while North Korean citizens were controlled by their government.

Let's look at the results. In North Korea, 2.5 million people don't have enough to eat. You can find photos of North Koreans on the street, bent over from malnutrition. Their government has starved them, resulting in incredible poverty.

Contrast that with South Korea. The Central Intelligence Agency ranks South Korea as 40th in the world, as measured by per capita GDP. Meanwhile, North Korea has fallen to a very low 197th. What's the difference between these nations? One has freedom while the other has slavery.[7]

This case study brings a central Godonomics principle to life:

- The greater the freedom, the greater the wealth.
- The greater the government, the greater the poverty.

A government is always a consuming part of the economy, since it does not produce. It cannot create profit and savings; it can only borrow by taxing the producers, inflating the currency, and/or enslaving its future through debt owed to other nations.

TAXATION SCALE
Percent the Producer Keeps

Slavery   Economy   Freedom

0%   25%   50%   75%   100%

The scale is the first aspect of liberty, and it points back to a fundamental difference between Jesus and Karl Marx. Marx didn't believe in individual property rights. Jesus affirmed them. Marx believed we should give to each one according to his need, while Jesus taught us to "settle accounts" based on faithfulness to stewardship and work (see Matthew 25:14–28).

Christianity and Marxism answer the basic question of life in directly opposite ways. Here is a snapshot of the opposing worldviews:

In his book *The Victory of Reason,* Rodney Stark traces the Christian roots of private property back to the beginning of Christianity. He notes that Christ-followers such as Augustine and Thomas Aquinas gave their sanction to private property, profit, and interest. In the thirteenth century, Albertus Magnus, a Christ-follower, wrote that a "just price" was "simply what 'goods are worth according to the estimation of the market at the time of sale.'"[8]

COMMUNIST MANIFESTO VS. THE BIBLE

Karl Marx (*Communist Manifesto*)	God (The Bible)
Who is God? (Atheism): God is a delusional lie.	Who is God? (Trinitarian Theism) God is the ultimate personal Truth.
What is truth? (Naturalism) Only matter exists; spirit is a nonexistent delusion. Truth is known only through the five senses.	What is Truth? (Supernaturalism) Both matter and Spirit exist and can be known through reason, experience, and supernatural revelation.
What is right/wrong? All truth is relative and determined by humanity. (There are no absolutes, except the absolute that all truth is relative.)	What is right/wrong? The Truth will set you free and is rooted in the character of God. (Truth is absolute and is revealed through creation and supernatural communication.)
Who are we? (Behavioralism) Humans are a highly evolved animal and are inherently good; in need of a good environment to stimulate good behavior.	Who are we? (Mind/body dualism) Humans are spiritual and physical beings made in the good image of God, but possessing a sinful heart that makes us individually responsible for our evil behavior.
How society works. Structure in society can be achieved by prioritizing the state, which creates the ideal environment by eliminating the corrupting influences of God, family, church, and individual rights.	How society works. Structure in society can be achieved by prioritizing God first; then the family, the church, the individual; and then the state as a protector of self-evident truths and individual rights.
How to govern. Since the individual is good but negatively impacted by his environment, the group trumps the individual in its need to create	How to govern. Since the individual is an eternal being and made in the image of the Creator, she is infinitely more valuable than

the ideal environment. The call for a totalitarian government is necessary to eliminate bourgeois ideology and capitalistic tradition until utopia can be reached.	the state. The role of the state is to protect the rights of the individual. Since humans have evil hearts, a society must be built on the rule of law, checks and balances of power, and an emphasis on liberty.
Economics. (Socialism) Since modes of production are the foundation for society, societal ills are caused by the emphasis on individual property rights and capitalism's imperfect emphasis on production. The group must abolish individual property rights and destroy capitalism.	Economics. (Stewardship of property through free-market capitalism) Property rights, incentive, individual responsibility, and liberty drive economics. A system that appeals to self-inter-est, and which allows people to bless others to profit, accounts for humanity's good and evil desires.

For more on the contrast between Marxism and Christianity, see David Noebel, *Understanding the Times* (Eugene, OR: Harvest House, 1994). More information can also be found at the Summit Ministries website, www.summit.org.

Jesus affirmed property rights in Matthew 25:14–15, in a parable about God and economics: "For the kingdom of heaven is like a man traveling to a far country, who called his own servants and delivered his goods to them. And to one he gave five talents, to another two, and to another one, to each according to his own ability; and immediately he went on a journey."

Notice that the man (representing God) gave property to his servants. They had a responsibility to make wise use of the property. Notice as well that God did not give to each person according to the person's need. He instead gave according to each person's *ability*.

The story gets more bizarre. At the end of the parable, two servants produced and profited, and they pleased God. God wants us to profit and to use the profits to invest more in helping others and in His kingdom endeavors.

Now, the story takes a final twist that would make Karl Marx turn over in his grave: God will give more to those to whom He had already given the most! The final servant who only had one talent didn't profit. Out of fear and laziness, he buried the talent.

> Then he who had received the one talent came and said, "Lord, I knew you to be a hard man, reaping where you have not sown, and gathering where you have not scattered seed. And I was afraid, and went and hid your talent in the ground. Look, there you have what is yours."
>
> But his lord answered and said to him, "You wicked and lazy servant, you knew that I reap where I have not sown, and gather where I have not scattered seed. So you ought to have deposited my money with the bankers, and at my coming I would have received back my own with interest." (Matthew 25:24–27)

God wants us to reap where we have not sown. He wants us to use our lives, opportunities, and talents to produce profits. God then affirms His desire for results by rebuking the lazy servant. God tells this servant that he could have at least put the money in the bank to collect interest. Then the God-character of Jesus's story does something almost unthinkable. He takes the property this servant had been given and gives it to the first servant, the one who had been given the most to begin with.

Jesus is not teaching us to take from the poor and give to the rich, but He is saying, "Take from the unproductive and give to the productive." In other words, "Take from the lazy and give to the hard worker." In the parable, God says to the sluggard, "Take the talent from him.... From him who does not have, even what he has will be taken away" (Matthew 25:28–29). Ouch!

What is Godonomics teaching us in this story? Liberty, hard work, and capitalism are rooted in Christian thinking. Throughout time, the scale of liberty has been championed by followers of Christ. The more you are able to keep and disburse from the fruit of your work, the more liberty you enjoy. This takes us to the second aspect of liberty, which has to do with the purchase.

What Would God Say to Karl Marx About Third-Party Purchases?

Why price and quality hold the secret to efficiency

There is a law of economics that transcends social and political systems. It is the reality of three different types of purchases: a first-party purchase, a second-party purchase, and a third-party purchase. Purchases built on a foundation of wisdom will result in prosperity, while purchases made with waste and foolishness lead to poverty (see Proverbs 24:3–4).

How does a proper understanding of purchasing result in riches and prosperity? The second aspect of liberty is the purchase. Let's begin by looking at first-party purchases.

First-Party Purchases

When I buy a product or service that I will consume and I'm using my own money, I care about price and quality. Let's say you and I meet for lunch at a sandwich shop. Immediately, an internal evaluation tool kicks in. "How much is it (price)?" and "Is this meal worth the price (quality)?"

If it's a twelve-inch submarine sandwich costing five dollars, you and I figure we can split the thing and each pitch in two fifty, plus the cost of two drinks. Feeling that a lunch for two fifty reflects the quality of the product, I'm all in.

First Party Purchases: I pay for something <u>with My Money</u> for services or products I will <u>consume for Myself</u>.

Second Party Purchases: I pay for something with <u>Someone Else's money</u> for services or products <u>I will consume for Myself</u>. Or <u>I pay</u> for something with <u>My Money</u> for services or products <u>Someone Else will consume</u>.

Third Party Purchases: I pay for something with <u>Someone Else's Money</u> for services or products <u>consumed by Someone Else</u>.

Who can determine when the price and quality are right? Only the consumer. It is different for all of us. (You might be really hungry and want the full twelve-inch sub, and you might feel it's worth five dollars even if you're not splitting the cost with me.) Other circumstances can affect your assessment of price in light of quality. You may say, "I'm willing to pay a certain amount for an umbrella during a rainstorm but far less on a sunny day." Only the buyer can determine the best price and quality.

Quality and price drive free-market capitalism. The seller must put the buyer's interest first. If a seller produces a product that the buyer determines costs too much or isn't of decent quality, the seller won't make money. But by catering to the needs of the buyer, a seller can make a profit. When a buyer freely chooses to buy a product, there is no such thing as an unfair price.

This first-party purchasing system produces the most prosperity in a nation and functions on the principle of liberty.

Second-Party Purchases

A second-party purchase takes place when the buyer cares about only one of the two factors involved in a purchase. Either you buy a product with your own money, but you will not consume it; or you consume it, but you bought it with someone else's money. When this happens, you are more flexible with one of the two purchasing factors. You are willing to compromise on price or quality, either because someone else is buying or someone one else will end up using the product.

My grandmother was a master of second-party purchases. She was extremely thrifty, to the point that she had a room in her house filled with gifts for others. She had shelves labeled "Gifts for men," "Gifts for children," and "Gifts for women." These were things she would never consume herself, but products she purchased at low prices to give away.

She would buy a dozen pink curtains at Big Lots to give to her daughters-in-law. She saw hunting knives on sale, five for ten dollars, and she bought all five without noticing the cracks in the blades. The quality was irrelevant to Grandma because she would not be using the items.

When Christmas came around, Grandma would stuff her cheap gifts into giant stockings and hand them out. We'd pull junky items from our stockings, and then the real fun began. Grandma's living room turned into a laboratory for free-market capitalism! An uncle might offer to trade his superhero blanket for my aunt's pink curtains. She might refuse that deal unless he threw in the pair of leggings he'd opened as well. The family was bartering until the quality of the trades was even.

One year my mother opened some pajamas that looked nice until she discovered they had wings like Batman's in the early comic books. She tried to be nice and say, "Thanks, Mom. This is wonderful!" And to this day, Batman-winged pj's given to my mother form my mental image of a second-party purchase. Of course, my family enjoyed the fun of the bartering system every Christmas. But it was obvious that all my grandmother cared about was price. She didn't care about quality since she would never consume any of the purchases.

The other type of second-party purchase occurs when I consume the product but don't pay for it with my own money. My favorite thing to order at T.G.I. Friday's is a banana strawberry smoothie. I'm willing to pay five dollars for this drink since I enjoy the taste and the quality. To you, it might seem to be a waste of money, but I have a right to my dessert preferences.

Let's say I am about finished with my smoothie, which I paid for out of my own funds. The server comes over and asks, "Would you like another one, sir?" I decide that while I was happy to pay five dollars for one, I am not willing to pay ten dollars for two. But then the server says, "Refills are complimentary." "Oh, well then… I'll take two." This now becomes a second-party purchase. If I don't have to pay for it with any more of my money, I am delighted to consume a second smoothie.

In instances of a second-party purchase, less care is taken in decision making. Either the consumer cares a little less about the price, or he cares a little less about quality.

And here is why second-party purchases are a problem. It is impossible to keep costs down and quality up when people are consuming items using someone else's money. The buyers face no adverse consequences if they give in to indulgence. In a second-party purchase, there are no pocketbook pains from overspending. Proverbs 6 makes this connection. After Solomon shows the importance of creating an antlike culture that rewards hard work and savings, he shows the problems of a sluggard economic system. He warns readers of the corruption and ruin that follow the sluggard (see Proverbs 6:6–15).

Solomon pointed out that laziness leads to wickedness as a society finds ways to cheat the system. In any second-party purchase, where a sluggard can consume without gathering his own food, he "devises evil continually" (verse 14). The result of all that evil mooching is that "calamity shall come suddenly" (verse 15).

Third-Party Purchases

The final type of transaction is a third-party purchase. It occurs when you buy something with someone else's money for a product or service that you will not consume. I heard former Congressman Bob McEwen illustrate the third-party purchase using a story about a stuffed green frog. Imagine that your boss penalizes employees ten dollars when they show up late for meetings. At the end of the year, the boss hands you the accumulated fines from the late-arrival jar and asks you to buy a prize that will be raffled off at the staff Christmas party. You now have three hundred dollars to spend on a nice prize. Over lunch, you hurry to a shopping mall, and at a toy store, you notice a giant stuffed frog. It stands four feet high and sells for two hundred ninety dollars.

You decide the frog will give everyone a laugh and will make a great prize for the party's raffle. You spend the three hundred dollars (not out of your own pocket) and buy the prize (which will belong to someone else). Normally, you'd never agree that a stuffed frog is worth three hundred dollars. But in this situation, you're in a hurry and are not personally invested in the transaction.

Both cost and quality were sacrificed, since the buyer was not heavily invested in the purchase. If you're wondering how this relates to Karl Marx, here is how: all government purchases are third-party purchases.

Governments use your money to purchase goods and services that someone else will consume. As the government's involvement increases, the waste increases and quality declines. It's the nature of all third-party purchases. During the healthcare debate of 2009–10, notice that members of Congress made themselves exempt from the program. If it's such a great plan, why would senators and representatives not want to sign up? As long as the decision makers provide services they will not consume, they keep their distance.

Why did Ronald Reagan say of the Berlin Wall, "Tear down this wall"? Because people in the eastern sector of the city didn't want to stay inside and enjoy the "benefits" of their communist government.

In a free-market system, entrepreneurs work overtime envisioning new products that will benefit customers. They take into account consumers' needs and the right price and quality of products that will meet those needs.

The more we focus on others, the more we benefit in the process. Both the consumer and the seller or producer profit. This process adds to a business's savings, which can be invested in expansion and job creation. With increased profits, a business owner is motivated to give to more people in need.

We began to understand what God would say to Karl Marx as we looked at the first aspect of liberty, the scale (in chapter 13). We have just looked at the three types of the purchase, which is the second aspect of liberty. Now let's examine the third aspect, the worldview.

The Third Aspect of Liberty: The Worldview

The way you think about life is your worldview. Your underlying assumptions about God, reality, humanity, and truth become the glasses through which you see everything around you. Small areas overlap as you compare various worldviews, Christian and otherwise. But far more frequent, and important, are the differences, which are startling.

You can reduce the most widespread worldviews into two major camps: atheistic and theistic. The first, atheistic humanism, assumes humanity is the standard of right and wrong, good and evil, ethics and morality, value and importance. The second major worldview, theism, begins with the assumption that God sets the standard that determines everything else.

HUMANISM AT A GLANCE

Humanism
The individual is good.
A person's environment is responsible for his or her behavior.
The individual is the standard.
Rights are granted by the group.

If your worldview places confidence in humanity as the standard, then by definition humanity is basically good. It follows that when individual humans do bad things, it must be because of their environment. If we can create the right environment for everyone, human behavior will be good. Applying this humanistic worldview to the political realm, we assume that if we can elect the right people and get them doing the right things, humanity's inherent goodness will prevail.

The weakness in this theory is that you can't find this model working, as designed, at any time in history. Consistently, throughout time and in every civilization and culture, humanity's natural tendency is to steal, lie, cheat, kill, deceive, and exploit.

The assumptions of humanism can be traced to a philosophy called Modernism. Thinkers such as Charles Darwin, Friedrich Nietzsche, and Karl Marx himself taught that education and enlightenment would remove society's need for God, freeing humanity from the binding limitations of religion. Prior to this, though religions and thinkers had differing assumptions about which truths were from God and which were not, everyone had traced truth to God, not humanity. By removing the linchpin of God from the dominant worldview, even Nietzsche realized that the consequences would be unthinkable. In 1882 he wrote,

> "Whither is God?" he cried; "I will tell you. *We have killed him*—you and I. All of us are his murderers. But how did we do this? How could we drink up the sea? Who gave us the sponge to wipe away the entire horizon? What were we doing when we unchained this earth from its sun?… Is there still any up or down?…
>
> "How shall we comfort ourselves…? Must we ourselves not become gods simply to appear worthy of it?…
>
> This deed is still more distant from them than most distant stars—*and yet they have done it themselves.*"[1]

Nietzsche's parable may be one of the most accurate predictions made during that time period. He realized that disconnecting right and wrong from God was like "unchaining this earth from its sun." Humanity without God would leave no fixed point to determine right from wrong. This philosophy is called Humanism.

OPPOSITE STANDARDS OF RIGHT AND WRONG

Humanism	God's Worldview
The individual is good.	God is good, and every individual needs a Savior.
A person's environment is responsible for his or her behavior.	Each person is responsible for his or her own behavior; one's environment has nothing to do with behavior.
The individual is the standard.	God is the Standard.
Rights are granted by the group.	Rights are granted by God.

In contrast, the theistic worldview was accepted by almost every religion and philosophy prior to the Enlightenment. It remains the worldview held by most religions today. Despite the fundamental differences between Islam, Christianity, and Judaism, they share a theistic worldview.

God is the standard. In this model, God is good, God is kind, God is generous, and we are not. No amount of environmental stimuli can cause or repair humanity's internal corruption. We have empirical evidence of this. Wickedness comes out of humans in rich as well as poor societies, educated and uneducated civilizations, and technologically advanced as well as primitive environments. We are not in need of a better environment but in need of God. We need someone to not only give us a path but to teach us how to walk in it. We need a Forgiver and a Leader.

A biblical worldview placing God as the standard means the individual, not the environment, is responsible for one's behavior. And one day, God will hold each of us individually accountable. This worldview is important to Godonomics because it elevates the necessity of accountability and responsibility.

Marx's Worldview Is the Enemy of Liberty

In Marx's humanistic worldview, humanity is god and humanity defines what is good.

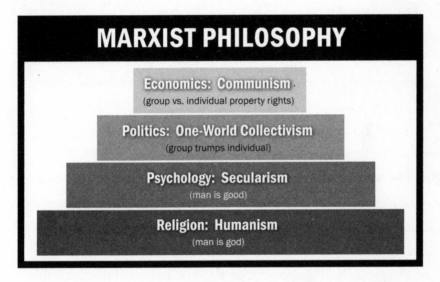

Marxism builds an irrational view of psychology by proposing the inherent goodness of humanity in spite of centuries of history showing that betrayal, hatred, violence, and injustice are the norm. Then Marx extends the irrationality into his political theory: the group trumps the individual. The greatest expression of human wisdom is the collective.

The individual is subservient to the society, hence the term *socialism*. Rights don't come from God to an individual, but from the collective (those in charge) to whomever they choose. With the collective in charge, it is also in a position to take away individual rights. The difference between socialism and free-market capitalism could not be more at odds. A socialistic society believes the state trumps the individual. A free-market society believes the individual trumps the state. Socialism believes the individual should serve the state, while capitalism views the state as the servant and protector of individuals' rights.

Marxism is bad economic policy built on inaccurate psychology and backward theology. The outcome is less liberty, less prosperity, less generosity, a huge government, a giant debt, and a downward spiral of morality.

In trying to figure out what God would say to Karl Marx, we need look no further than America's Declaration of Independence. America's founders based the new nation's governing principles on a set of truths. Thomas Jefferson penned, "We hold these truths to be self-evident, that all men are created equal, that they are endowed by their Creator with certain unalienable Rights." Jefferson's self-evident truths are a colonial way of saying, "Any idiot should be able to see this!" But today's cultural trend rejects ideas such as truth and self-evident and inalienable rights.

The founders further clarified the purpose of government when they wrote in the Declaration, "That to secure these rights, Governments are instituted among Men, deriving their just powers from the consent of the governed."[2]

The people hold the power, choosing to loan limited powers to the government. Taxpayers hold the government accountable, since power lies ultimately with the people. Contrast that with Marx's socialism, which wields power to threaten (and kill) citizens who refuse to cooperate with the government's "greatest good."

The pursuit of happiness goes hand in hand with liberty, which brings us back to the scale that we looked at in chapter 13. The slave is burdened with more government, resulting in less personal wealth. The free person is blessed with less government and the freedom to keep more of his money.

We were created out of the mind and image of God. Humans have inherent value and rights simply because they are created by their Heavenly Father, who grants them dignity and value.

What does this have to do with Godonomics? Throughout history we can trace a cycle that many nations have followed. Most great civilizations last no more than two hundred years. We were not founded as a simple democracy, but as a democratic republic, the first one in history to build its foundation on this theistic worldview. America has already outlived the typical two-hundred-year destiny. Nations with a godly worldview begin with a period of great prosperity as they follow God's principles. This is followed by a period of apathy. In their apathy, they turn away from God, resulting in God's judgment.

The book of Judges illustrates this cycle. We see in Judges a description

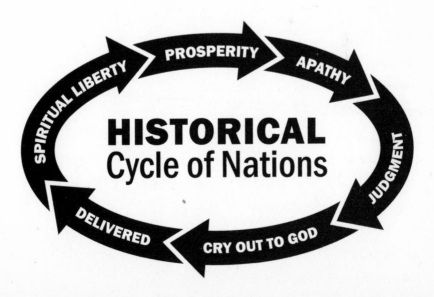

of three hundred fifty years of Israel's going through the cycle again and again. The cycle reoccurs over seven times. Each time, after the people turned from God, He reveals what a merciful and gracious God He is. He takes them back. He heals their land. God walks with them on the road to recovery.

In the story of the Cross, we see a God who not only sees our brokenness but takes our brokenness upon Himself. He takes the punishment that we deserve and gives us the freedom we could never earn. He then gives us a new worldview, a new way of blessing others with liberty, prosperity, and generosity.

PART 8

If God Were Talking to the Internal Revenue Service

What Would God Say to the IRS About Voluntary Giving?

The powerful impact of purposeful, heartfelt generosity

Certain dates evoke emotion in each of us. A personal favorite is the fourth Thursday of November, a day of gratefulness. Family members come from all over the Midwest to indulge in the gluttony. They bring dozens of dishes, including pies, cakes, casseroles, and turkey. We laugh and play games until the inevitable comatose nap at 2:30.

And the following month there is Christmas. December 25. Ahhh. Feelings of generosity envelop the room as we sit around the Christmas tree, eagerly watching as one family member at a time opens gifts!

What comes to mind when we mention October 31? For me, Halloween candy heads the list. I think of all the neighbors who give out generous amounts of sugar treats to children dressed in ridiculous costumes. Not only do the kids appreciate October 31, but their dentists also have reason to give thanks.

But then there is April 15. A day filled with giving but rarely with cheer. Few of us rejoice as we share what we have with a distant institution in Washington. The giving that takes place every April is coerced by law. Taxpayers have no choice but to help finance government projects, whether they support the causes or not.

These four dates reveal the different emotions associated with giving. Cheerful giving, which characterizes the events that take place on three of the dates, softens the heart. But the giving that is done on April 15 most often hardens the heart. Far from exercising our free choice to give away a portion of our wealth, we are forced to give. The Bible addresses these two ways of giving, showing the problems that result from an excessive tax system.

An Excessive Tax System Punishes Liberty

At issue when we talk about a national income tax is the question: should government promote more liberty or more control? Raising tax rates to increase government revenues feeds centralized control over individuals, whereas reducing taxes allows citizens to take responsibility for caring for themselves and others. The choice is control or liberty.

This might not be the first thing that comes to mind, but an ancient king's experience in Israel can help us sort through this issue. Rehoboam held a cabinet meeting that is described in 1 Kings 12.

The king's father, Solomon, had led Israel to unprecedented success. Solomon was known for his building projects, national prominence, and influence that reached far beyond the region the nation occupied. Initially, the Israelites revered their king. However, over time, Solomon's popularity faded due to higher taxation and more government control. Following Solomon's death, the people were ready for a new administration. All of Israel came out to cheer on their new leader (see 1 Kings 12:1).

The nation had been divided over partisan battles. Now Israel was embroiled in civil war, setting the northern tribes against the southern, Israel vs. Judah. However, the transfer of power from Solomon to his successor king was a potential time for change—for peace. King Jeroboam, the leader of the northern tribes (Israel), who had been in exile, approached Rehoboam, who was in command of the southern kingdom (Judah). He pleaded with Rehoboam to reunite all the tribes and, to get that done, to guarantee a return to liberty.

> Jeroboam and the whole assembly of Israel came and spoke to
> Rehoboam, saying, "Your father made our yoke heavy; now therefore,
> lighten the burdensome service of your father, and his heavy yoke
> which he put on us, and we will serve you." (1 Kings 12:3–4)

Jeroboam reminded the king of Judah that such a course of action would result in greater love and service to him, not less. Rehoboam must have wondered if granting Jeroboam's requests would cause him to look like a failure for decreasing the size of government. And what about all the projects he had dreamed of completing?

The king called together his cabinet members, who were divided on the best way to proceed. Some who had served in his father's administration had seen the consequences of Solomon's policies. These older, wiser, and more mature advisors gave him this advice: "If you will be a servant to these people today, and serve them, and answer them, and speak good words to them, then they will be your servants forever" (1 Kings 12:7).

This is a blueprint for the way leaders should serve their constituents. "If you serve them, they will serve you. Speak good words to them, and you will have their hearts forever." In other words, lighten their load. Giving citizens more liberty and individual responsibility leads to increased prosperity and, therefore, greater loyalty to the king or government.

But Rehoboam, like many leaders, sought additional input, seeking advice that was more to his liking. He "consulted the young men who had grown up with him, who stood before him. And he said to them, 'What advice do you give?'" (1 Kings 12:8–9).

The second group of advisors had not been in the trenches with King Solomon. They lacked the wisdom of experience, and they sided with

Rehoboam. In modern words, they replied, "More control! More power! Show them who's in charge!" Because these young men were in the governing class, they wouldn't be impacted by their own advice (see 1 Kings 12:10–11).

Sadly, Rehoboam decided to add to the burdens of the people. He opted for even more coercion at the risk of never reuniting the nation's warring tribal coalitions.

This sounds a lot like politics in America, where leaders choose to not listen to the people. The outcome is that citizens are hurt by the ideas and policies of the governing class.

In ancient Israel, the more that Rehoboam tried to control the people, the more popular support he lost. He should have adhered to the words of God, the elders who had served Solomon, and perhaps that great line spoken by Princess Leia to the Death Star's commander in *Star Wars:* "The more you tighten your grip, Tarkin, the more star systems will slip through your fingers."[1]

The problem with a large government and excessive taxation is that it diminishes liberty because it is both punitive and partial. God condemns the perversion of justice, by favoring some over others. "For the LORD your God is God of gods and Lord of lords, the great God, mighty and awesome, who shows no partiality nor takes a bribe. He administers justice for the fatherless and the widow, and loves the stranger, giving him food and clothing" (Deuteronomy 10:17–18).

A Progressive Tax Policy Is Punitive and Selectively Unjust

Godonomics is built on the impartial rule of just laws. Everyone is treated and judged the same—regardless of socioeconomic status. Does this sound like common sense? It's the difference between a democracy and a republic. A republic is a government system based on laws (like our Bill of Rights) that protect the minority from being oppressed by the voting of the majority.

Those laws protect the minority from a voting majority that might choose to violate the minority's civil rights, property rights, or God-given rights to life, liberty, or the pursuit of happiness.

In a democracy, a majority of voters could vote to deport all left-handed people. If you could get a majority to vote for this action, it would be enacted as law. In a republic, however, the majority can never take away God-given rights no matter how large the majority that favors such action. Even in America's republic, where representatives are elected to vote on proposed legislation, the representatives swear to uphold laws, rights, and the constitution, which imposes limits on each branch of government.

Today in America, rich people are taxed at a higher rate than the middle class and the poor. They also are demonized, blamed unjustly for causing the ills of society. Sadly, the common belief is that higher tax rates on the rich are both fair and a moral sense of social justice.

Taxation, like other laws, must be based on impartiality and be rooted in the moral law of God. As Martin Luther King Jr. said in his letter from an Alabama jail, "A just law is a man-made code that squares with the moral law or the law of God."[2]

An unjust law is a code that is out of harmony with the moral law. According to St. Thomas Aquinas, "An unjust law is a human law that is not rooted in eternal law and natural law."[3]

This truth applies to the guarantee of equal access to justice no matter who you are, what socioeconomic class you are part of, or what race or ethnic group you belong to. If the federal tax code exacts a greater financial penalty against those who realize a higher income, it is unjust.

We need wise, selfless leaders whose philosophy is rooted in moral law. Today, when a political leader endorses moving the tax code toward equality, progressive politicians attack the proposal with "We gave a $2 million dollar tax break to industry, and only a $200 tax break to the middle class. That's not fair!"

Let's examine that faulty rationale. If Person A makes $100,000 and pays 10 percent in taxes, she gives $10,000 to the government. If Person B makes $10,000 and pays ten percent in taxes, he sends $1,000 to Washington. But let's say a new law enacts a flat tax for taxpayers at all income levels, and the new rate is 9 percent. Person A would save $1,000, while Person B would save only $100. Progressive politicians would attack such a change, charging that it is unfair to the taxpayer who earns less and, thus, saves less in tax liability. The truth is this: it's not unfair, it's just math!

Americans suffer a far greater inequality due to the severely unjust progressive tax rate. The top 50 percent of America's wage earners pay 96.54 percent of all the income-tax revenue collected in the United States. The top 1 percent pays more than one-third of the entire IRS collections at a tax rate of 34.27 percent. Despite this inequality, most uninformed voters remain unruffled by the unjust government leeching.

Far worse is the fact that an ever-increasing percentage of persons B, with an income below a predetermined level, pay nothing. But they receive an income-tax credit in the form of a check when they did not pay anything into the system. The federal government uses unjust laws to steal from Person A and give to Person B, and *everyone* gets hurt.

When you increase taxes on the top earners using disproportionate tax rates—rates that increase as you make more money—it results in unintended negative consequences for the poor. Profitable businesses cover the cost of higher taxes by increasing the prices of their products, forcing a hardship on all consumers. And businesses recover the business cost of higher taxes by enacting certain economies, including laying off workers. The wage earner at the lower end of the income spectrum loses his job and descends into poverty, because the high-income producer was taxed unjustly.

There are proposals to make tax policy just by enacting a flat tax or fair tax. Many economists and think tanks have shown that a flat tax would have several benefits. The Heritage Foundation outlined some of the advantages.

- Revenue Neutral: The new [flat] tax system should be revenue neutral, raising as much revenue as current policy—about 18.5 percent of the economy....
- Three Deductions [Allowed]: The only remaining deductions are for higher education, gifts and charitable contributions, and an optional home mortgage interest deduction....
- Saving Is Tax Free: Personal saving would be deducted immediately and would remain tax exempt until [the money is] spent on consumption....
- Straightforward Transition: Current arrangements would be grandfathered, subject to current law, and the New Flat Tax would apply to new income....
- Higher Wages, Stronger Companies: The New Flat Tax means higher wages and more competitive companies through increased private investment.[4]

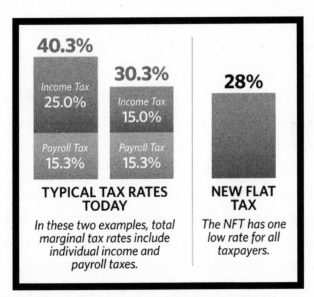

40.3%

Income Tax
25.0%

Payroll Tax
15.3%

30.3%

Income Tax
15.0%

Payroll Tax
15.3%

28%

TYPICAL TAX RATES TODAY

NEW FLAT TAX

In these two examples, total marginal tax rates include individual income and payroll taxes.

The NFT has one low rate for all taxpayers.

Sources: Heritage Foundation calculations and the Internal Revenue Service, 2011 Tax Rate Schedules. Used with permission.

The rule of law means everyone is under the same standard. When God put in place His principle of revenue generation for His people, it was based on a percentage. This meant that all the people were under the same law. Whether you were rich, poor, foreigner, or citizen, the law was the same. The various proposals on flat taxes and fair taxes seem to be much more in line with God's standards, and they make more economic sense than a progressive system. Notice the flat, fair, consistent standard God uses with the tithe:

> When you have finished laying aside all the tithe of your increase in the third year—the year of tithing—and have given it to the Levite, the stranger, the fatherless, and the widow, so that they may eat within your gates and be filled, then you shall say before the Lord your God: "I have removed the holy tithe from my house, and also have given them to the Levite, the stranger, the fatherless, and the widow, according to all Your commandments which You have commanded me; I have not transgressed Your commandments, nor have I forgotten them." (Deuteronomy 26:12–13)

Note as well God's commandment to apply the same law equally to everyone: "One law shall be for the native-born and for the stranger who dwells among you"—and applied equally to both the king and ordinary citizens (Exodus 12:49; see also Deuteronomy 16:18–20; 17:18–20).

God knows the human heart can only experience liberty, prosperity, and genuine generosity by giving freely. He also instructs that if the laws of a society are to be just, they will be anchored in the just laws of His nature, like an impartial, equally applied standard that all people are held accountable to.

There are two types of giving that are seen prominently in the religious and political realms through history. Let's examine the two methods: the Begrudging/Coercion Method and the Generous/Conversion Method.

Giving Begrudgingly: Forcing and Coercing

A group of men meet weekly to study the Bible at my church. Some are new to biblical principles, some are skeptical, and some are already very familiar with the Bible. I poked my head into the room last week as they were studying the book of Romans. Paul had told the Christians living in Rome to be honest and law abiding and to pay the taxes required of them. One man in the study group jokingly said he wondered what Paul could have been thinking. Another mentioned that Jesus told His disciples to pay Caesar what was due him (see Romans 13:7; Matthew 22:21).

Jesus and Paul taught respect for the law. They said Christians should obey laws and submit to authorities, even when the governmental authority at that time was the evil emperor Nero or Trajan. Christ-followers paid the taxes they owed, even while refusing to worship the emperor. The lives of early Christians were threatened, and yet they refused to compromise. They held fast to their convictions and worshiped God alone.

History reveals a unique dichotomy of conviction and boldness, combined with respect and humility, on the part of those who followed Jesus. While we are to respect the laws of the land, we can never forget that God alone is God. We owe our first allegiance always to God. And Christ-followers are taught in the New Testament to work toward a better way. We are to seek a different way of giving and a different way of living.

The IRS forces you to give away your money. In contrast, Jesus invites you to give away your money. Coercion hardens the human heart, while Jesus's way softens it. Godonomics is about charitable generosity, while socialism is about coercion.

Economist Milton Friedman rightly called socialism a force. It forces someone to do something they wouldn't do if they had a choice. Coercion in any form stands in opposition to the Bible's call to an inside-out transformation of individuals and society.

Taxation involves two types of coercion.

Political coercion

In *The Interesting History of Income Tax,* William Federer marks the development of the US income tax.

- In 1787 the US Constitution prohibited a "direct" federal tax.
- In 1862 a "revenue tax" (another word for income tax) was "temporarily" levied on incomes to finance the Union during the Civil War.
- In 1895 the US Supreme Court declared the income tax unconstitutional.
- In 1913 an income tax of 1 percent was levied on the top 1 percent of income earners.
- In 1943 the federal government required employers to withhold a portion of employees' pay to help finance World War II.[5]

Federer's book describes John F. Kennedy's proposed tax plan, which aligns closely with what is emphasized in Godonomics. It's a new way of thinking about economics. Kennedy said the following when he came into office: "Lower rates of taxation...will stimulate economic activity and so raise the levels of personal and corporate income as to yield within a few years, an increased...flow of revenues to the Federal Government."[6]

It is counterintuitive to argue that lowering the tax rate will result in increased tax revenue. But Kennedy and others since have advanced this plan, and it is backed up by sound economic theory, not to mention being consistent with the Bible's requirement for just laws.

Lower tax rates will produce more producers, which will expand business, production, and employment. This produces more profits as well as bigger payrolls. With more savings being realized by businesses and individuals alike, more capital will be available for investment, leading to entrepreneurial expansion, which will produce even more jobs, which creates even more taxpayers. Even at a lower tax rate, a bigger pool of taxable income will generate more government revenue.

Kennedy's statement to Congress was later depicted by Art Laffer in what is known as the Laffer Curve. The Laffer Curve demonstrates that there is a point in city, state, and federal governments that the higher tax rates rise, the less revenue is collected.

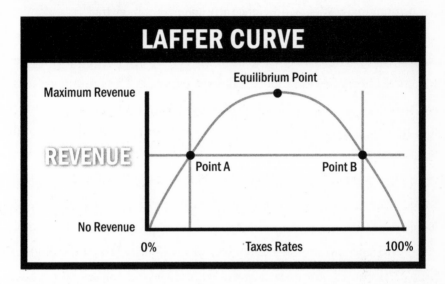

As tax rates rise, those who have capital sit on it rather than investing it. Tax collections drop off because fewer investors are willing to pay the tax penalty. High-tax-rate states lose businesses to states where tax rates are more attractive.

Religious coercion

We can't talk about generosity and giving without looking at religious coercion. The church has historically been just as involved in coercion as the government. In fact, Paul addresses this in his second letter to the Christians living at Corinth.

> Prepare your generous gift beforehand, which you had previously
> promised, that it may be ready as a matter of generosity and not as
> a grudging obligation....
>   So let each one give as he purposes in his heart, not grudgingly or
> of necessity; for God loves a cheerful giver. (2 Corinthians 9:5, 7)

Notice that Paul instructed giving on an individual basis as each person determines, without pressure. Individualism is the pattern supported in the Godonomics model. Paul further admonished giving that is done cheerfully, not begrudgingly. What a difference attitude makes in giving!

Religious coercion uses fear and an appeal to people's pride to force compliance with a religious agenda. Some church leaders play on our lack of scriptural knowledge to produce a desired response. Their threats produce fear that moves us to give, but begrudgingly. Religious leaders through history have taught a coercive message of "If you don't give, God will punish you."

They also appeal to people's pride and arrogance. When I was in college I sometimes gathered with a group of friends to mock religious coercion. We would watch television evangelist Robert Tilton appeal to his viewing audience's arrogance by offering them a way to manipulate God. He would tell people, "If you will just make a vow of faith, then God will send you a huge sum of money."

Who are we to tell God what He has to do? Who are we to think we can issue a command to the Maker of the universe?

None of our financial giving and no amount of good works can make up for our sins. Yet religious coercion plays to that idea by suggesting that we can buy our way into God's favor. God has made it clear that only through Christ can we deal with our sin problem. Only seeing what Christ has done for us can change our hearts. That is the difference between begrudging giving and cheerful giving.

Many times the beauty and wonder of the gospel message is not painted clearly enough so that all people see what God has done and what He can do for us. In the New Testament, Paul wrote, "Therefore I thought it necessary to exhort the brethren, that they would go before unto you, and make up beforehand your bounty" (2 Corinthians 9:5, KJV).

You may ask, "What is the motivation to give?" Paul provides the answer: "Every man according as he purposeth in his heart, so let him give; not grudgingly, or of necessity: for God loveth a cheerful giver. And God is able to make all grace abound toward you; that ye, always having all sufficiency in all things, may abound to every good work" (verses 7–8, KJV). God's grace is the motivator. You realize what you have in Christ and what He has done for you. That is when you begin to look at your money and say, "I can use this money as a seed to *invest* in God's work." Our real eternal riches are never going to disappear.

We should give as a response to how Christ gave to us (see 2 Corinthians 8:9). If you want to access real riches, you must look to Jesus Christ. He came from the glory of God, which holds a million multiplied by a trillion times more riches than anything you have ever imagined. The things we hunger after (comfort, security, peace, joy, love) were things Jesus enjoyed in heaven with God. Yet He pushed that aside to come to earth.

With the incarnation of Christ, God's world came into our cursed, broken world.

Jesus came to offer us a way to come back into His world. When the way of grace is not just some prayer you prayed years ago but is a reality in your life, you say, "I want to give to others in response to how He gave to me." If He could be that generous to me, the least I can do is to be more generous— radically generous—toward others.

This is why, in the wisdom of Godonomics, giving is motivated by grace. God gave us gifts and opportunities to produce so we can leverage our productivity in celebration and gratefulness to Him.

By God's grace and power, I want to make a profit. I want to save. I want to give to others as He has given to me. I want to invest in others like He invested in me. When we begin to understand these things, our embittered hearts begin to soften.

The gospel of Christianity differs from the coercion of socialism and organized religion. The gospel changes you from the inside out. Organized

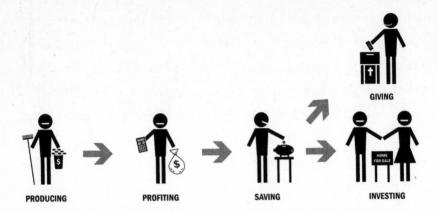

religion, and the socialist economic model, attempt to control you from the outside in.

The problem with trying to be good enough for heaven is that you run out of deeds that are good enough—and numerous enough—to compensate for your bad deeds. The solution is grace. The act of receiving it is as simple as saying a prayer like this to God:

"Jesus, thank You for giving up Your riches. Thank You for being willing to live on earth in poverty. Thank You that through Your sacrifice, I can be adopted into God's family. Come into my life now. [Or, You have been in my life, but I have put myself on the throne, and now I want You to get back on the throne.] I give up trying to make myself good enough. I am humbling myself and asking for Your forgiveness and grace. Be my King. Be my Savior. Rescue me from myself and the punishment of an eternity without You, so I can live with You eternally. Amen!"

If God Were Talking to You and Me

What Would God Say to Us About Political Involvement?

Here are the best reasons for getting involved

Jotham hid in a corner while mercenaries killed seventy of his brothers. Before the slaughter ended, almost all of his family members had lost their lives on a giant stone in the middle of the city of Shechem.

This was no random act of violence. Jotham's brother Abimelech had hired gangsters to eliminate others in the family line who might rise up to challenge his claim to national leadership. It was known that kings of neighboring pagan nations had killed off family members to protect their royal claims. But until now, Jotham had never seen a judge of Israel resort to fratricide just to consolidate his rule over a nation (see Judges 9:1–5).

After the slaughter, Jotham stood up in a public forum and related a parable—a fable—about a forest that was desperately in need of leadership.

> The trees once went forth to anoint a king over them.
> And they said to the olive tree,
> "Reign over us!"
> But the olive tree said to them,
> "Should I cease giving my oil,
> With which they honor God and men,
> And go to sway over trees?"

Then the trees said to the fig tree,

"You come and reign over us!"

But the fig tree said to them,

"Should I cease my sweetness and my good fruit,

And go to sway over trees?"

Then the trees said to the vine,

"You come and reign over us!"

But the vine said to them,

"Should I cease my new wine,

Which cheers both God and men,

And go to sway over trees?"

Then all the trees said to the bramble,

"You come and reign over us!"

And the bramble said to the trees,

"If in truth you anoint me as king over you,

Then come and take shelter in my shade;

But if not, let fire come out of the bramble

And devour the cedars of Lebanon!" (Judges 9:8–15)

When good people are too busy to serve in leadership and public office, the thorn bush (in this case, the evil Abimelech) takes command. Jotham was calling his fellow citizens to get involved in the realm of governance and politics. "The forest is burning down! People are dying all around you, and the trees are too busy to care. You must not be like these apathetic trees!"

In the fable, the trees and the vine were so consumed with their own lives and work that they couldn't be bothered to serve, to lead, or to help. So the people ended up with a bramble in power.

In the United States, good people are too busy to lead and to stand for what is right. In addition to constant overscheduling, Americans have been brainwashed into believing that godly people shouldn't be involved in politics. Or in a similar vein, it's suggested that godly people will be corrupted and turn away from God if they are actively involved in political causes. Now many of us who have not been involved in the public forum are seeing the results of our absence.

We need instead to educate ourselves and then take action. We need to inform our neighbors and friends and become part of the solution.

In Jotham's fable, the trees were so desperate for leadership that they invited a thorn bush to be their king. Jotham calls this new leader a bramble bush, which his audience would know was used as kindling to start cooking fires in the wilderness. The thorn bush told the trees, "Okay, I'll be your king. But on one condition: you have to take shelter in my shade" (see Judges 9:15). Shade? A thorn bush does not cast any shade. It's a broken, flammable bush! There is no comfort there, no real protection from the burning sun.

As the trees' leader, the thorn bush manipulated them, promising that he would burn down the forest if they didn't get on board with his program. In fear, the disengaged trees agreed to let the thorn bush run the kingdom. The trade-off was that they would be free to return to the woods where they could mind their own business.

It was the same thing the people of Shechem had been doing, or not doing. Jotham screamed at the apathetic citizens, and it's the same challenge that he is screaming at you and me: "Get out of the woods! Stop ignoring the flames!"

Today, Americans are like the trees that stay in the woods, taking care of their own lives while the forest is being ignited. The forest is headed for disaster, but the trees can't be bothered to do anything to help.

Too many pastors teach their congregations about the Bible's guidance in marriage, parenting, evangelism, and other areas while overlooking God's teachings on how nations are to operate according to His will. Why do

American Christians pretend that Congress and the president are capable of hammering out a plan for the nation's economy that will get everything back on track?

Economic systems are not merely a matter of personal preference or something to be left up to the ruling political party. God stands squarely behind the principles of free enterprise and capitalism. He makes it clear that a free-market economy and decentralized government is the only combination of economic and political systems that consistently open the way to opportunity, prosperity, and appropriate financial reward while guarding against the abuses of unchecked central authority, which reward sloth, greed, and corruption.

We have already looked at what God would say to philosophers, economists, national political leaders, and social-justice Christians. Now we will turn our attention to what God has to say to you and me about taking responsibility.

Convictions and Protection

To begin to reverse the slide and redirect our nation back toward its founding principles and God's wisdom, we need to restore two things that are lacking: convictions and protection. We will look first at convictions, which are the courage to do what's right as God defines right.

Convictions

Jotham acted on conviction when he challenged the people of Shechem. His father, Gideon, also known as Jerubbaal (a nickname he got for tearing down the Baal idols from his father's home), fought for the people. The men of Shechem remembered the oppression of the Midianites and Gideon's reluctant—yet courageous—leadership. They knew Jotham's father had fought and almost died to bring liberty to Israel. They knew the battle stories describing the terrible price that was paid for them to be free from Philistine bondage.

So Jotham challenged the people, saying, "Remember my father. He didn't ignore the flames! He was a man of conviction. But what about you? Are you operating in truth and sincerity? What is driving you: your convictions or your fears?" (see Judges 9:16–20).

It takes conviction to step into the mudslinging public square, knowing your intentions will be misconstrued and your children might pay a price as a result of your outspokenness. But the alternative is to stand aside and watch the forest burn down. Taking action is what being salt and light is all about. Jesus calls us to saturate and to penetrate our culture. We need to have the conviction to face down our fears and get out of the woods!

This brings us to protection, the second of two missing essentials that needs to be restored. Jotham addressed this second essential in his challenge to the people of Shechem.

Protection

Jotham was being hunted by Abimelech's men because of his opposition to the would-be dictator's murderous agenda (see Judges 9:21). The story of Jotham and his courageous acts can shake us out of our apathy. We are called to stand up for the rights to life, liberty, and the pursuit of happiness. These God-given rights must be protected.

Christ-followers must not turn deaf ears to the urgent call to fight economic evils: the evil of stealing from one group to give to another, the evil of political corruption in a union boss, the evil of exploitation in a CEO, the evil of companies—such as Bear Sterns, Fannie Mae, or AIG—asking the government to bail them out while enslaving our children with debt payments on the borrowed money. Christians have an allegiance to a higher kingdom of truth. We must not stand for the corruption or injustice of any leader, no matter what political allegiance the leader might claim. Where will apathy lead us if we choose to continue to not act?

As I approached the opportunity to write this book, it was out of a sense that the culture needed to know God's wisdom on economics. Knowing that

American politics can be so divisive, I dove into the project with fear and trembling, yet convinced that Americans desperately needed Godonomics!

I've always loved this statement by C. S. Lewis: "Christianity has not, and does not profess to have, a detailed political programme for applying 'Do as you would be done by' to a particular society at a particular moment. It could not have. It is meant for all men at all times and the particular programme which suited one place or time would not suit another."[1]

As much as I agree that the Bible doesn't give a detailed political program, I know that the Bible *does* give us clear, unwavering principles for thinking through any public policy. As I studied the Jotham passage in the book of Judges, I was convicted that I need to get involved in a more intentional way. I, too, complain about our country. I complain about politicians. I complain about the economy. Yet I remain too busy and too disillusioned to heed Jotham's warning and get out of the woods. I hear Jotham shouting to me, just as he is shouting to you: "If you have acted in truth and sincerity… let him also rejoice in you. But if not, let fire come from Abimelech" (Judges 9:16, 19–20).

Do you have the courage to do what's right as God defines right, as well as the concern for justice as God defines justice? Will you protect the innocent? Will you stand up for the oppressed? Will you act according to your moral convictions?

Jotham's refrain is "if you have done right." Let's ask ourselves, "Is it right to try to live insulated in the woods while innocent people are dying?" His voice is haunting: "Just wait, the flames are coming. They will burn down the village with you in it. You can't ignore the danger, the evil and corruption. You can't hide forever."

A Jotham-type voice during World War II was Pastor Martin Niemöeller (1892–1984). He spoke about the inactivity of German intellectuals and clergy following the Nazi rise to power. "First they came for the Communists, but I was not a Communist so I did not speak out. Then they came for the Socialists and the Trade Unionists, but I was neither, so I did not speak out. Then they came for the Jews, but I was not a Jew so I did not speak out. And when they came for me, there was no one left to speak out for me."[2]

Pastor Niemöeller and Jotham were both correct. When leadership gives in to evil, the flames destroy innocent lives. America is on the same trajectory as Nazi Germany and ancient Israel in the time of the judges! We must be the generation that steps up to the plate to restore honor to God and our public leadership.

It's amazing how much God can accomplish with men and women of conviction. Centuries ago, one monk and a Christ-follower stopped the violence of the gladiators. Early in the fifth century, a monk from Asia Minor named Telemachus was led by a mysterious inner voice to go to Rome. He went there without knowing why and followed the crowds to the Colosseum. Two gladiators were fighting, and Telemachus tried to get between them to stop them. Three times he shouted, "In the name of Christ, forbear!" One of the gladiators thrust a sword through him, yet he continued shouting. Those watching the spectacle were angry that the monk had interrupted the games. In a rage, the crowd began throwing stones and other instruments into the ring, trying to silence Telemachus.

A short while later, Honorius, who inherited the empire of Europe, put a stop to the senseless violence of the gladiatorial combats. Honorius's decision traces back to the speech and spectacle of one monk's courageous stand. Honorius counted Telemachus a victorious martyr for ending the impious spectacle and the taking of innocent life.[3]

Where do we get the courage to go outside our comfort zone? Where will we find the boldness to respond? Look deeply to the One who got out of the woods Himself. Jesus was enjoying the cosmic delight of heaven, yet even then He didn't ignore the flames. He saw the evil in our world and chose to not stay home. He took on the thorn bush of evil. He faced the stings of Satan. He allowed His Father to pour out the flames of judgment on Him.

Jesus felt the torture of a mock trial. He suffered the crushing blows of the Roman and the Sanhedrin political structures, both vying for power and trampling His body in the process. Despite the torture and shame, Jesus went into the flames to rescue us. Jesus's finished work of atonement and redemption challenges us to get out of the woods and speak His truth with conviction. In light of what He's done for us, we must do the same for others. When we see Jesus Christ for who He really is, we will take the necessary risks to act when we see others in need. We will see our nation in trouble and choose to get out of the woods. We will stop ignoring the flames!

Our choice is to act or to not act. We can choose to continue complaining while doing nothing to right the wrongs, or we can become actively involved in public life. If Christ-followers fail to act, the thorn bush will continue to rule the forest.

Jotham's story challenges us to proclaim God's kingdom while living in the kingdom of earth. Jotham challenges us to live out daily the prayer "Thy kingdom come, thy will be done in earth, as it is in heaven" (Matthew 6:10, KJV). There is no room for apathy or indifference.

Now more than ever, we need people of conviction who are willing to stand for justice. We need champions to step forward to valiantly protect our inalienable rights of life, liberty, and the pursuit of happiness. America is on the edge of the flames. Feel the heat! Take a stand, and take action to spread the truth.

What Would God Say to Us About Planning?

Seven steps to help you and your
family put Godonomics to work

People often want to pray their way out of situations they have behaved their way into. As they see trouble looming, they engage in more and more magical thinking. They hope God will rescue them from the consequences of unwise decisions and a lack of planning.

God is clear when He tells us that borrowing leads to enslavement. We can ignore His warnings and pretend that our situation is an exception to the rule. We can tell ourselves that being enslaved to creditors will not create excess stress in our lives and relationships, including our marriages. But saying these things doesn't make them true.

Here is a good rule to start with when seeking to follow God's wisdom regarding personal and family finances: direction, not intention, determines destination.

The decisions you make today, and the actions you take based on those decisions, will determine where you end up in a year, five years, ten years, twenty-five years, and beyond. You are headed in a particular direction spiritually and financially. If you make the wrong choices now—decisions that will aim you in the wrong direction—you will not like it when you arrive at the destination.

I can't count the number of people who have sat in my office, telling me they had no intention of losing their spouses, their families, their businesses.

They had no plans to ever have an affair, to neglect their kids, or to get so deep into debt that they couldn't get out. They had not heeded God's wisdom to plan in advance to achieve the outcome they desired. And by ignoring God's words, they failed to realize that their intentions were irrelevant. They made choices that pointed their lives in a particular direction, and now they had reached the destination.

The same is true for you, for me, and for our country. No member of Congress intends to bankrupt the United States. But they do want to be re-elected. Few national leaders intend to do things that increase the rate of unemployment, but they end up pushing for policies that achieve that unwanted result. You and I can't control the federal government, no matter how much we would like to. But we can control our own decisions and actions. We can choose the things that will orient us in the right direction. Let's look at several ways to act now, so that in time we will arrive at the desired destination.

Financial Directions You Can Count On

God wants you to experience liberty, productivity, and generosity. To arrive at that destination, you need to take action now that will buck the tide of national economic trends. For eight years, President George W. Bush followed the advice of John Maynard Keynes. Immediately following that, President Barack Obama adopted the same advice, which has continued to move the United States in the same direction, only with greater speed. Sadly, on the national level, the destination is clear. We are headed to a painful destination financially. But as individuals and families we can decide now to head for a different financial destination.

Direction #1: Produce more

Your family will be better off with multiple streams of income. As we have seen, Godonomics begins with production. In today's economy, there is no such thing as job security. Years of loyalty to your employer count for nothing. Production is the answer, and that is why you need multiple streams of income.

This is important for a number of reasons. Even if you don't lose your job, you can make good use of a second revenue stream. The added income can be used for savings, to pay down debt, and to increase your generosity. And if you should lose a job, you have positioned yourself to continue producing. Your second income stream is already in place. This will be invaluable as you seek new employment.

Generating multiple income streams can be as basic as using an interest, technical specialty, talent, hobby, or area of expertise in a gainful fashion. I started playing soccer when I was five years old. I learned to referee soccer when I was twelve. Back then I earned four dollars per game. Today, referees who work at children's soccer games in our area make ten dollars an hour, minimum, and as much as twenty dollars an hour. The stress level is low, especially if you are refereeing the younger age groups.

My son has been refereeing for two years, and sometimes we do it together. I am using this area of expertise—which coincides with an interest that Javan and I share—to help him learn a good work ethic, responsibility, and the critical importance of production in financial well-being. He is learning to work, save, and give.

My daughter and I walked into a Texas Roadhouse restaurant several months ago. A balloon artist was there, making balloon animals for the kids. I introduced myself and asked if she needed additional balloon artists. She said she did, and soon my teenage daughter and I were working at birthday parties once a month. This is another revenue stream, and even better, I get to do something fun and productive with my daughter. (This could easily become a business if we wanted to develop it more.)

Discover your passions. Learn new skills. Try new things. You never know what you may be good at. Look at your hobbies, and dream about how to turn them into revenue generators. My dad and I started a blacktop-sealing business when I was a teenager to make money to buy our first boat. I am teaching my son to use eBay to sell the mountain of Legos he no longer uses. Look around you; there is money to be made.

Direction #2: Spend less

My children love thrift stores. We are regular customers at Goodwill stores, since one person's garbage is another person's gold. Plus there is a sense of adventure when you shop at thrift stores. You never know what you might find.

Even if you have multiple streams of income, it is necessary to keep your expenses down. Consolidate debts from multiple credit cards into one payment, and then cut up the cards. Stop eating out. Sell the stuff you are storing in the attic or garage. Turn the thermostat down in the winter and up in the summer. Or in the summer, open the windows and use fans. Cancel your cable or satellite TV. Live without a cell phone, or at least without a smart phone.

I know that cutting back on things that are considered necessities is a radical step. But spending less than you make is a nonnegotiable.

If you want to save, invest, and give, you need to practice saying, "We can't afford it." There is great freedom in these four words. Sure, you could drive a newer car, go on a cruise, buy more toys. But when you prioritize the things God values—saving, investing, and giving—you choose to not afford certain other things. Another way to say, "We can't afford it" is to say, "It's not a priority." Make spending less the inviolable priority until your revenue and spending are in alignment.

Direction #3: Build up an emergency fund

Jesus made it clear that we will have tribulation (see John 16:33), so now is the time to prepare for trouble. As you make a practice of spending less than you make, set aside savings. Use the savings to build up an emergency fund, and don't touch it unless there is a real emergency. That means a crisis such as the loss of a job, a major roof repair, or a major medical expense. Set aside a percentage of your income for this fund, and resist the temptation to tap into it until it is really needed.

My Grandpa Eltrevoog was disciplined with his emergency-fund money. He left it untouched so it would be there in case of emergency. He also used it as a reserve fund to help people. There were times when relatives would pull Grandpa aside and share some difficulty they were going through. He would disappear and return with a hundred dollars or more to give them.

When he died, we cleaned out his house and found five thousand dollars stashed in cracks, corners, and boxes all over the house.

Experts recommend setting aside the equivalent of six months of income. How do you get there? One step at a time. Start with a goal of five hundred dollars, then increase your goal to one thousand dollars. Begin the process now, and work toward reaching the destination.

Direction #4: Reverse the snowballing of debt

Your debts will escalate unless you take decisive action to pay them off. So get out all your credit cards. Then determine which one has the lowest balance. Create a monthly budget that frees up money to pay down that debt first. Pay it off as quickly as possible, then do the same with the next-higher balance. You will benefit from the sense of accomplishment you experience from paying off the first card, which will energize you to pay off the next card balance. The snowball effect of aiming money that had been unproductive (paying interest on purchases of items you stopped using years ago) to productive (freeing you from debt once and for all) is a powerful force.

When you pay off the balance on the last card, do not make the mistake of assuming that money is now available to be spent. Put that money into savings, for your emergency fund and for investment and giving. Reversing the snowball effect will work only if you work at it.

Direction #5: Don't lose sight of savings and investment

Once you have set aside an emergency fund equal to six months' income, start building up savings for the longer haul. Devote at least 15 percent of your income to a Roth IRA or other retirement plan. You should also use

savings to prepare to pay for your children's college expenses and other looming expenses that you can see on the horizon.

As you save for future expenditures, don't fall for the sure-thing investment. For instance, housing is a big gamble. Even investment opportunities
such as a rental properties can fail to provide a reasonable return on your investment. So be very conservative in your assumptions about tomorrow as
you plan and invest.

Direction #6: Remember that trajectory is everything

We live in a broken world that will never come close to being perfect. So we
need an approach that will aim us in the right direction to get us to the desired destination. It takes time and discipline, and there will be setbacks along
the way. So find the thing that will keep you on track. I suggest the word
trajectory.

We will never save, budget, or spend perfectly, but we do want to be on
the right trajectory—the one that will move us steadily toward achieving
these goals. Our direction determines our destination. If our planning is
characterized by aiming in the direction of Godonomics, we will keep moving toward God's chosen destination for us.

Are your financial habits characterized by godly, wise decisions? If they
are, there is a great destination ahead. If not, you will keep lying to yourself,
or you will attempt a change for a short while and then give up.

Remember, your intentions are irrelevant. No one sets out to fail, but a
lot of us end up failing anyway. Your direction and trajectory are the things
that determine your destination. If you intend to save, but you keep overspending instead, you will not have any savings to cover the needs that will
be sure to come up, much less have anything for retirement.

There is pain in our future, in large part because our country is on the
wrong trajectory. So prepare now. Even if the economy were to suddenly turn
around, the practices of wise financial management will still get you out of
debt and position you for financial health and stability. We will probably

never return fully to a constitutional, limited republic, but we must vote for candidates and policies that shrink deficit spending, enhance private industry, reward and incentivize work, and cut government spending.

Direction #7: Teach children to be producers

We need to teach our children the skills—not just the theory—that will lead to their success as adults. I am indebted to my grandparents and parents for instilling these practices in my life in memorable ways. However, most parents today assume that parents are the producers and their children are, by default, consumers. That may be true when the children are very young, but as kids grow from preteen to adult, parents must begin turning children into producers.

Parents do that by giving their children increased responsibilities to go along with new freedoms. Assign them work, teach them to save for a car or college, and make sure they learn to write checks and balance a checkbook. From age eleven on, my children have earned money doing odd jobs. Out of their profits, they put 10 percent into a giving jar and 10 percent into a saving jar. These are some of the habits and skills that will set them up for a successful, others-focused life.

A Life-Changing Trajectory

When I was twenty-one, I realized that my budget revealed my actual priorities. While I said God was a priority, none of my money went to support my church. I was an active volunteer in many of the church's programs to help people who were struggling, but my money was staying home. I told myself it was appropriate to be giving of my time rather than my treasure. I reasoned that I was newly married and poor. We needed every penny.

Still, although I was not helping to fund programs in the inner city, I was able to buy a four-in-one game set from Sharper Image.

Beth and I were newlyweds living in Chicago, and we could afford very little. We rented the cheapest apartment we could find. Its four hundred square feet included a kitchen, pantry, and living room—pretty much all the same room. We couldn't fit Beth's waterbed into the bedroom so we slept on a twin. Our bathtub was about thirty inches long.

One day I was trying to take a bath, and Beth walked in. I had my feet up in the air so I could get my back into the warm water. She said something pithy like, "Did I really marry you?"

We joked about the dinky apartment and our meager finances. But I had just finished a video project for a client and had received a check for four hundred dollars. Of course, I headed to the mall, wondering what I would spend it on. That's when I visited Sharper Image.

It's almost impossible to walk through Sharper Image without coveting. I'd noticed the four-in-one game table before. It was about four feet by three feet. It had a miniature pool table, Ping-Pong table, and hockey table, as well as a place to play chess and other board games. I really needed that game table.

Remember, we were poor newlyweds. We needed something with which to have fun. And Beth agreed to the purchase. The good news is that I had saved the money for it, so we didn't go further into debt. But wow, what a terrible idea!

I brought the four-in-one game set home and put it together in the living room. Get up from the couch and you'd run into it. Walk around the TV, you'd run into it. Finish eating and look over there and all you could see was couch, TV, and game table. The floor was not visible.

It was an all in one, all right. It became our kitchen table, our coffee table, and our junk drawer—all in one.

It's important to mention that we had an artificial Christmas tree. The only place to set it up was on the four-in-one game table. You'd think the message would have gotten through to me at that point. But I felt we still needed something more. We couldn't get any television stations on our small

TV, so I called my dad and said, "Dad, if you need some hints for my Christmas list, we could use an antenna."

I figured he might get us a twenty-dollar Radio Shack antenna. On Christmas he said, "I got something that's perfect for you." I wasn't prepared for how perfect it was.

My dad is the king of thrift. He found a deal on one of those giant antennas that you see mounted on the roof of a house. He drove to Chicago from Peoria, got out of his truck, and walked into our tiny apartment with our present.

So now we had a giant, three-foot-tall, five-foot-wide antenna sitting on top of our TV. Granted, we could get more stations now, but that Christmas we had to get rid of the Christmas tree on the game table and decorate our antenna instead.

Even though we were poor and had a very limited income stream, a sense of discontentment still drove me—and it drove me to make really dumb decisions. It was time to analyze my spending. I decided that giving to God and His work needed to become a precedent, beginning with a budget that "told my money where to go." I couldn't look at my checkbook register and say it represented the way I wanted my heart to operate.

Our first budget was formed as I began resisting the temptation to remain undisciplined. The decision to stop doing things the same way I had in the past, and to make changes that would get our finances in line with God's will, changed my life and our finances as a couple.

Beth and I were determined to not spend more than we could afford, but we didn't want to cook in our tiny apartment during a steamy Chicago summer. So we got creative.

My dad found a used window-unit air conditioner at a garage sale. It worked a little in the sense of cooling one room down several degrees. The only window in our apartment was in the bedroom. The only way the bed fit into the small room was against the window. At the risk of oversharing, the smallness of the bedroom meant that I was sleeping with the air conditioning right at my buttocks, and it froze into a block of ice at least once a week. It was a cold night's sleep through the summer of my first year of marriage.

We look back on those days as challenging but fundamental to our financial path. We chose budgeting over borrowing. The net result? We are more financially free today because we chose to get on a different trajectory early in our marriage. We refused to make the bad exchange of borrowing rather than budgeting.

We have done our best to live according to the principles of Godonomics and to teach them to our children. Let's all commit ourselves to be models of these principles: to produce, to profit, to save, to give, and to invest. Let's show our children and the world a living example of Godonomics vs. Meonomics. We can save this country one life at a time, one family at a time, and one community at a time.

NOTES

Chapter 1: It Is No Accident That God Endorses Capitalism

1. William Bradford, *History of Plymouth Plantation* (Boston: Little, Brown, 1856), 74, 78, 80, 91.

2. For more on this, see *The Founders' Constitution*, vol. 1, chap. 16, doc. 1. (Chicago: University of Chicago Press), http://press-pubs.uchicago.edu /founders/documents/v1ch16s1.html/. See also William Bradford, *Of Plymouth Plantation, 1620–1647*, ed. Samuel Eliot Morison (New York: Modern Library, 1967).

3. *Star Trek II: The Wrath of Khan,* directed by Nicholas Meyer (Los Angeles: Paramount Pictures, 1982).

4. C. S. Lewis, *Mere Christianity* (New York: Macmillan, 1960), 74–75.

Chapter 2: What Would God Say to Adam Smith About Work?

1. D. James Kennedy, *What If Jesus Had Never Been Born?* (Nashville: Thomas Nelson, 1994), 117.

2. Kennedy, *What If Jesus Had Never Been Born?*, 118.

3. Adapted from a portion of "Social Injustice," Snopes.com, www.snopes .com/college/exam/socialism.asp.

4. Adam Smith, *The Theory of Moral Sentiments* (1759; Indianapolis: Liberty Classics, 1984), 241.

5. Smith, *Theory of Moral Sentiments,* 82–83.

6. Kennedy, *What If Jesus Had Never Been Born?,* 107.

7. Julian the Apostate, Letter 22, "To Arsacius, High-Priest of Galatia," in Flavius Josephus, *Works,* trans. W. C. Wright, The Loeb Classical Library, 10 vols. (Cambridge, MA: Harvard University Press, 1926), 3:2-235, www.tertullian.org/fathers/julian_apostate_letters_1_trans .htm.

8. Adam Smith, *An Inquiry into the Nature and Causes of the Wealth of Nations,* ed. S. M. Soares (Lausanne: MetaLibri Digital Library, 2007), 16, www.ibiblio.org/ml/libri/s/SmithA_WealthNations_p.pdf.

9. Sam Ro, "Milton Friedman's Brilliant Response to Phil Donahue's Question About Greed," *Business Insider,* July 31, 2012, www.businessinsider.com/milton-friedman-on-greed-2012-7, with an embedded link to the interview, www.youtube.com/watch?v=RWsx1X8PV_A/.

10. Smith, *Wealth of Nations,* 417–18.

Chapter 3: What Would God Say to Adam Smith About Profit?

1. Arthur Brooks, *Who Really Cares: The Surprising Truth About Compassionate Conservatism* (New York: Basic Books, 2006), 50. "Religious liberals bear a resemblance to religious conservatives in their giving habits. They are almost as likely to give (91 percent), but give away about 10 percent less money than religious conservatives each year. On both of these measures, they greatly exceed population averages. They are about as likely to give to secular causes as religious conservatives. Two-thirds volunteer each year. They are a bit less likely than religious conservatives to volunteer for religious causes, and a bit more likely to volunteer for nonreligious causes. The bottom line for charity on the nexus of politics and religion is this: Religious people are far more charitable than secularists, no matter what their politics. But while religious conservatives are common, religious liberals are a fairly exotic breed. Liberals are far more likely to fall in the "secular" category than the "religious" category, and this is one big reason liberals as a group tend to look uncharitable."

2. John C. Maxwell, *Ultimate Leadership: Maximize Your Potential and Empower Your Team,* Christian Leadership Collection (Nashville: Thomas Nelson, 2007), 132.

Chapter 4: What Would God Say to John Maynard Keynes About Spending?

1. David Pietrusza, interview by Glenn Beck, *Glenn Beck,* FoxNews, August 13, 2010, www.foxnews.com/story/0,2933,599523,00.html#ixzz2BMFOonL7.

2. USDebtClock.org, http://usdebtclock.org/index.html. National debt statistics current as of February 9, 2013.

3. This quote is found in many sources. Here are a few of them. John Maynard Keynes, First Baron Keynes of Tilton (June 5, 1883–April 21, 1946), quoted in "Whose Mercy?" Time magazine, February 17, 1947. "Before his

death, Lord Keynes had spoken his mind about those sterling debts: 'If you owe your bank manager a thousand pounds, you are at his mercy. If you owe him a million pounds, he is at your mercy.'" Also quoted in Paul Bareau, The Future of the Sterling System (London: Institute of Economic Affairs, 1958), 26: "If you owe your bank manager £1000", he (Keynes—ed.) used to say, "you are at his mercy. If you owe him £1000000 he is at your mercy."

Chapter 5: What Would God Say to John Maynard Keynes About Budgeting?

1. Alexander Eichler, "Paul Krugman: Job Loss Under Bush Much Worse Than Under Obama," *Huffington Post,* April 23, 2012, www.huffington post.com/2012/04/23/job-loss-obama-bush_n_1446650.html. For additional insight about job losses in the private sector since 2000, see Michael Mandel, "A Lost Decade for Jobs," *Business Week,* June 23, 2009, www. businessweek.com/the_thread/economicsunbound/archives/2009/06/ a_lost_decade_f.html.

2. "Don't Buy Stuff You Cannot Afford," *Saturday Night Live,* NBC, February 4, 2006, www.hulu.com/watch/1389.

3. For more on these ideas see Rodney Stark, *The Victory of Reason* (New York: Random House, 2005), 172.

4. To read more about building margin into your life, I recommend Richard Swenson, *Margin: Restoring Emotional, Physical, Financial, and Time Reserves to Overloaded Lives* (Colorado Springs, CO: NavPress, 2004).

5. Howard Dayton, *Your Money Counts: The Biblical Guide to Earning, Spending, Saving, Investing, Giving, and Getting Out of Debt* (Carol Stream, IL; Tyndale, 1996), 32.

Chapter 6: What Would God Say to FDR About Unintended Consequences?

1. To learn more about the David Walker movie *I.O.U.S.A.* (2009) from the Peter G. Peterson Foundation, go to www.youtube.com/watch?v=O_Tj BNjc9Bo.

2. Chris Edwards, "The Government and the Great Depression," Cato Institute, *Tax and Budget Bulletin* 25 (September 2005), 1, www.cato .org/pubs/tbb/tbb-0508-25.pdf

3. Edwards, "The Government and the Great Depression," 1.
4. Edwards, "The Government and the Great Depression," 2.
5. Edwards, "The Government and the Great Depression," 1. Original notes to source: U.S. Bureau of the Census, Historical Statistics of the United States, 1975, Part 1, p. 135. For the change in output during the 1920s, see U.S. Bureau of the Census, Part 1, p. 224. For unemployment, see p. 135.
6. Amity Shlaes, *The Forgotten Man: A New History of the Great Depression* (New York: Harper, 2008), 214, 220.

Chapter 7: What Would God Say to FDR About Budgeting?
1. R. C. Sproul Jr., *Biblical Economics: A Commonsense Guide to Our Daily Bread,* 3rd ed. (Powder Springs, GA: Tolle Lege, 2008), 72.

Chapter 8: What Would God Say to FDR About Liberty?
1. For more on this, see Amity Shlaes, *The Forgotten Man: A New History of the Great Depression* (New York: Harper, 2008).
2. "Bill of Rights," *The Charters of Freedom,* www.archives.gov/exhibits/charters/bill_of_rights_transcript.html.

Chapter 9: What Would God Say to Alan Greenspan About the Money Supply?
1. Alan Greenspan was appointed to office on August 11, 1987, by President Ronald Reagan and served until January 31, 2006, the fifth year of George W. Bush's presidency.
2. John Maynard Keynes, *Essays in Persuasion,* Section "Inflation and Deflation," paragraph titled "Inflation (1919)" (New York: W. W. Norton, 1963.

Chapter 10: What Would God Say to Alan Greenspan About Greed?
1. Peter Schiff, *Crash Proof 2.0: How to Profit from the Economic Collapse,* 2nd ed. (New York: Wiley, 2011), 14–18.
2. Ronald Sider, *Rich Christians in an Age of Hunger: Moving from Affluence to Generosity* (Nashville: Thomas Nelson, 2005), 32.
3. Ruth Moon, comp., "Are American Evangelicals Stingy?" *Christianity Today,* January 31, 2011, www.christianitytoday.com/ct/2011/february/areevangelicalsstingy.html.

Chapter 11: What Would God Say to Jim Wallis About Socialism?

1. *The Princess Bride,* directed by Rob Reiner (Los Angeles: Act III Communications, Buttercup Films Ltd., The Princess Bride Inc., 1987).

2. J. Strong, *Enhanced Strong's Lexicon* (Bellingham, WA: Logos Bible Software, 2001), s.v. *"mishpat."*

3. Milton Friedman, quoted in "Preface: Economic Freedom Behind the Scenes," in "Economic Freedom of the World 2002 Annual Report," Cato Institute, 2002, xvii–xviii, www.cato.org/pubs/efw/efw2002/efw02-intro .pdf.

4. Dave Workman, "What I Meant to Say. Really." *What I Meant to Say* (blog), April 15, 2011, http://daveworkman.blogspot.com/2011_04_01 _archive.html.

5. Thomas Aquinas, quoted in Russell Kirk, "The Meaning of Justice," lecture no. 457, *Heritage Foundation,* March 4, 1993, www.heritage.org/research /lecture/the-meaning-of-justice.

6. Julian Lamont and Christi Favor, "Distributive Justice," *Stanford Encyclopedia of Philosophy,* ed. Edward N. Zalta (Spring 2013), http://plato.stanford .edu/entries/justice-distributive/.

7. BusinessDictionary.com, s.v. "distributive justice," www.businessdictionary .com/definition/distributive-justice.html#ixzz2BYz52fvz/.

8. Stoyan Zaimov, "Hugo Chavez Thanks God, Promises More Socialism After Presidential Victory," *Christian Post,* October 8, 2012, www.christian-post.com/news/hugo-chavez-thanks-god-promises-more-socialism-after-presidential-victory-82888/#Vv6jtHwOF8kEFVvv.99.

9. Philip Sherwell, "Death of Hugo Chavez Could Set Off Shock Waves Across Region," *Telegraph,* January 5, 2013, www.telegraph.co.uk/news /worldnews/southamerica/venezuela/9782566/Death-of-Hugo-Chavez-could-set-off-shock-waves-across-region.html.

10. Ray Walser, PhD, "The Chávez Plan to Steal Venezuela's Presidential Election: What Obama Should Do," Heritage Foundation, September 19, 2012, www.heritage.org/research/reports/2012/09/the-chavez-plan-to-steal-venezuelas-presidential-election-what-obama-should-do#_ftn4/.

11. See Jim Wallis and Joyce Hollyday, "A Plea from the Heart," Advocate column, *Sojourners,* vol. 12, no. 3, March 1983, 3. Jim Wallis and a cowriter critiqued US involvement in Nicaragua. They wrote, "The cause of the

violence is the invasion of counterrevolutionary forces, or contras, from
Honduras into Nicaragua, who employ tactics of terror, torture, and
murder against the Nicaraguans who live in the frontier. The source of the
violence is the U.S. government, which has orchestrated and financed this
covert, and now overt war against Nicaragua. This action by the United
States is both illegal and immoral, but thus far all efforts in the United
States to change this destructive policy have gone unheeded." While Wallis
and I might agree on waste in military spending and overreach of the
American military, his position seems more than an economic perspective.
Wallis is a pacifist who rejects Jesus's affirmation of the ethics of war from
Deuteronomy as well as history's just war theory. However, despite his
pacifism and fair critique of the unstoppable spending of our government
toward war, Wallis seems to see the US government itself as immoral. This
perspective views the US government not as the good guys fighting the evil
of communism, but rather the bad guys who are "immoral."

12. Sara Pulliam Bailey, "Wallis Admits to Soros Funding," *Christianity Today*
(blog), August 20, 2010, http://blog.christianitytoday.com/ctpolitics/2010
/08/wallis_admits_t.html.

13. Trinity United Church of Christ, "About Us," www.trinitychicago.org
/index.php?option=com_content&task=view&id=20.

14. Trinity United Church of Christ, "About Us."

15. Of course, exceptions exist. Leading up to the Civil War, Christian clergy
in the South and elsewhere were some of the most vocal opponents of
emancipation. And more than a century later, during the civil rights
movement of the 1960s, Christians in the South—as well as southern
leaders in the Democratic Party—were active in opposing federal legislation and court rulings that outlawed segregation. Historically, it has been
political conservatives and Republicans who have fought for equality. While
some Christians were on the wrong side of this issue, the majority of
Christians—as well as the testimony of Scripture—has upheld the sanctity
of all life and defended the equality of all persons as bearers of God's image.

16. After John the Baptist was unjustly imprisoned, John's disciples came to
Jesus. John and they had proclaimed Jesus as Messiah and assumed he was
about to lead a political rebellion. As zealots, John the Baptist and his
disciples were looking for Jesus to show them how he would fulfill the Isaiah
61 passage about setting the captives free. They wondered how Jesus could

be the legitimate Messiah if he wasn't doing what the Messianic passage demanded. Jesus answers their question about his identity by quoting the Messianic passage from Isaiah 61. However, Jesus left out these words from Isaiah's prophecy: "...To proclaim liberty to the captives, and the opening of the prison to those who are bound" (Isaiah 61:1; cf. Luke 7:22). Jesus was letting John know (through John's disciples): "You are not going to get out of prison. The kingdom is not coming as a full political revolution against the Romans at the first coming. I am setting the captives free from death and fear through my upcoming death on a cross" (though Jesus didn't spell out the details of that here in this passage). What's interesting about his application is that Jesus quotes Isaiah 61 in its entirety in Luke 4:18–19 to reveal himself as the Messiah. So clearly, his omission of the phrase with John is intentional to clarify that the Messiah's kingdom and freeing of captives is not about physical restraints and political revolution.

17. Trinity United Church of Christ, "About Us."

Chapter 12: What Would God Say to Jim Wallis About the Rule of Law?

1. American pastors and theologians who support this view are not as prone as their European counterparts to use the word *Marxism*. American Christians know that citizens of the United States value the benefits of free enterprise and are familiar with the developments of the twentieth century. The Cold War is still fresh in the memory of most adult Americans.

2. This quote has been removed from most of the websites where it had been posted earlier. However, the following Media Matters link shows Glenn Beck screening the video clip in which Al Sharpton makes the statement. (It is interesting that Media Matters criticizes Beck for doing this.) See Fae Jencks, "Beck Distorts King's Legacy While Blaming Sharpton for Having 'Perverted' It," Media Matters for America website, July 17, 2010, http://mediamatters.org/research/2010/07/17/beck-distorts-kings-legacy-while-blaming-sharpt/167836.

3. Social Justice Definition website, www.socialjusticedefinition.com.

4. Jim Wallis, "How Christian Is Tea Party Libertarianism?" Sojourners, *God's Politics* (blog), May 27, 2010, http://sojo.net/blogs/2010/05/27/how-christian-tea-party-libertarianism.

5. John Adams, *The Political Writings of John Adams: Representative Selections*, ed. George A. Peek (Indianapolis, IN: Hackett, 2003), 148.

6. Wallis, "How Christian Is Tea Party Libertarianism?"

7. Cato Institute, "Economic Freedom of the World," www.cato.org /economic-freedom-world.

8. Jim Wallis's support for socialistic societies can be found in his writing for *Sojourners,* as documented in the research of David Noebel, of Summit Christian Ministries. For more on this, see David A. Noebel, "Barack Obama's 'Red' Spiritual Advisor," *The President's Desk* (blog), March 27, 2009, www.summit.org/blogs/the-presidents-desk/barack-obamas-red-spiritual-advisor/.

9. Tad DeHaven, "Why Is There So Much Government Waste?" Cato Institute, "Commentary," October 17, 2012, www.cato.org/publications /commentary/why-is-there-so-much-government-waste.

10. Ryan Messmore, "Obama Makes Fifth Attempt to Reduce Charitable Tax Deduction," *Foundry,* March 1, 2012, http://blog.heritage.org/2012/03/01 /at-it-again-obama-makes-fifth-attempt-to-reduce-charitable-tax-deduction/.

Chapter 13: What Would God Say to Karl Marx About America?

1. From www.summit.org/resources/worldview-chart. Used with permission.

2. I thank Congressman Bob McEwen for permission to use in this chapter some of the ideas and analysis from a speech he gave on socialism and capitalism. For more on this, go to http://bobmcewen.com/.

3. Thomas Jefferson, quoted in *The World's Great Speeches,* ed. Lewis Copeland, Lawrence W. Lamm, and Stephen J. McKenna, 4th ed. (Mineola, NY: Dover, 1999), 261.

4. Jarrett Skorup, "Detroit: The Triumph of Progressive Public Policy," *Michigan Capitol Confidential,* July 6, 2009, updated February 14, 2012, www.michigancapitolconfidential.com/12832/.

5. William McGurn, "Michigan's War on the Middle Class," *Wall Street Journal,* March 22, 2011, http://online.wsj.com/article/SB10001424052748 703858404576214931414415452.html?mg=com-wsj/.

6. Michael Barone, "Census Figures Show Detroit's Utter Devastation— Down 61 Percent Since 1950," *Washington Examiner,* "Politics," March 23, 2011, updated March 16, 2012, http://washingtonexaminer.com/article /142668.

7. Central Intelligence Agency, "The World Factbook," www.cia.gov/library /publications/the-world-factbook/rankorder/2004rank.html.

8. Rodney Stark, *The Victory of Reason: How Christianity Led to Freedom, Capitalism, and Western Success* (New York: Random House, 2006), 63, 65.

Chapter 14: What Would God Say to Karl Marx About Third-Party Purchases?

1. Friedrich Nietzsche, "The Madman," 1882, in Liliane Frey-Rohn, *Friedrich Nietzsche, Beyond the Values of His Time: A Psychological Approach to His Life and Work* (Einsiedeln, Switzerland: Daimon, 2012), 71.
2. The Declaration of Independence: A Transcription, www.archives.gov /exhibits/charters/declaration_transcript.html.

Chapter 15: What Would God Say to the IRS About Voluntary Giving?

1. *Star Wars,* written and directed by George Lucas (San Francisco: Lucasfilm and Los Angeles: Twentieth Century Fox Film Corp, 1977).
2. Martin Luther King Jr., *Letter from the Birmingham Jail,* http://mlk-kpp01 .stanford.edu.index.php/encyclopedia/documentsentry/annotated_letter _from_birmingham.
3. Thomas Aquinas, quoted in King, *Letter from the Birmingham Jail.*
4. The Heritage Foundation, "The New Flat Tax: Encourages Growth and Job Creation," Factsheet no. 98, January 19, 2012, www.heritage.org /research/factsheets/2012/01/the-new-flat-tax-encourages-growth-and-job- creation. Used with permission.
5. William J. Federer, *The Interesting History of Income Tax* (St. Louis, MO: Amerisearch, 2004), back cover, www.amazon.com/Interesting-History- Income-Tax/dp/0975345508.
6. John F. Kennedy, "Annual Budget Message to the Congress, Fiscal Year 1964," January 17, 1963, www.presidency.ucsb.edu/ws/?pid=9241.

Chapter 16: What Would God Say to Us About Political Involvement?

1. C. S. Lewis, "Social Morality," *Mere Christianity,* rev. ed. (San Francisco: HarperSanFrancisco, 2001), 82.
2. Leo Stein, *Hitler Came for Niemoeller: The Nazi War Against Religion* (Gretna, LA: Pelican, 2003), front cover, www.amazon.com/Hitler-Came- Niemoeller-Against-Religion/dp/158980063X.
3. Marianne Hering and Paul McCusker, *Attack at the Arena* (Wheaton, IL: Tyndale, 2010).

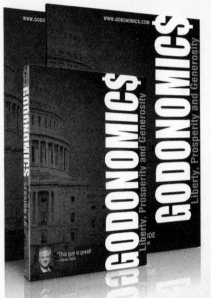